PLASTIC SURGEON MARKETING MOTTO

THE SECRET RECIPE TO GROW REFERRALS

PHILLIP GUYE • JOSEPH PRESTON

Doctor
Book
Publishing

Publisher of Plastic Surgeon Marketing Motto:
DoctorBookPublishing.com - An Imprint of Deep Think Media
1425 K Street, NW
Suite 350
Washington, DC 20005
1-800-704-3447

ISBN-10: 0982631340
ISBN-13: 978-0-9826313-4-8

DISCLAIMER
The information presented in this book is for educational and informational purposes
only. The authors and publisher of this book disclaim any loss or liability, either
directly or indirectly as a consequence of the information presented herein, or the
use and application of such information. This book is sold with the understanding
that the authors and publisher are not engaged in rendering medical advice, diagnosis
or treatment.

Printed in the United States of America.

The Plastic Surgeon Marketing Motto
According To Phillip Guye And Joseph Preston:

"Promote Unto Others So They
Will Promote Unto You."

www.PlasticSurgeonMarketingMotto.com

DEDICATION

I dedicate this book to Billy Ray Guye and Olga Petrovitch Guye the two people that: got up so early every morning providing for our family, so that I would not have to… worked such long hours and multiple jobs, so that I would not have to… kept warm winter coats on our backs, so that I would not have to… kept an endless amount of food on our plate, so that I would not have to… went without so many luxuries of life, so that I would not have to… put off their own personal dreams, so that I would not have to… risked losing everything, so that I would not have to… sacrificed so much of their lives, so that I would not have to…

believed in me no matter what the teachers said…
trusted me under any and every cir-
cumstance without question…
taught me the value of saying "Thank
you" and meaning it…
trained me to adore learning. It
was not easy, I know…
gave me a proper understanding of "respect for others"…
educated me on what is most important in life…
always say "as long as you're happy, we're happy"…
did not ever force me but guided me…
made my love of helping people possible…
set such an amazing example in my life
making failure completely impossible...
have given me what often feels to be
a unfair advantage in life...
I credit 110% of my success...
are my two lifelong heroes...
I am the most proud to call Mommy and Daddy.

I could not have done it without the both of you.
"Love" does not even begin to describe it...

Your very proud son,
Phillip Ray Guye

DEDICATION

I dedicate this book to my dear Mother and Father, two amazing people who help instill in me the passion to serve and help others.

Joseph Preston

"Anyone in the healthcare industry with an MD or an MBA after their name needs to read Plastic Surgeon Marketing Motto. Joe Preston and Phil Guye have created one of the most innovative referral and patient getting systems ever developed."

-Dr. Steve Vasilev, MD, MBA

"If you only read one book about marketing your medical practice this year, this is the one. Phil Guye and Joe Preston are authorities on how to influence and persuade prospects and convert them into patients."
-Dr. Kim Millman, MD, PhD

"I love passion and there is no one more passionate about what they do than Joe Preston and Phil Guye. And they are just dedicated to my success. And for me, not only do I want them to be successful but I want my friends to experience what Joe and Phil have done for me. The effort on my part was not even a blip on my radar screen. And the results have been phenomenal."

-Dr. Jason Stoner, DDS, MS

"Joe Preston and Phil Guye are the consummate professionals. They have really used their expertise in the areas of marketing and media training and media coaching to help me convey my message in the strongest way possible to my patients. I'm glad that we did because it really helps me to this day."

-Dr. David Scharf, DMD

"I couldn't say enough great things about Joe Preston and Phil Guye. I mean, in a really short amount of time, I feel like they are my long lost brothers. They are committed guys, hardworking much like myself, maybe that's why we connect. They are all about the bottom line and we need to get the job done no matter what it takes, we're going to get the job done and that's how I am. No matter how long the day is, we're going to get it done and we're going to make it right and we're going to make it happen and we're going to make it a success. So, I'm very happy and fortunate, really to have met them and connected with them and I'm very, very satisfied with their excellent, beyond excellent, service and expertise."

-Dr. Ed De Endrade, DDS

"Joe and Phil and their team were very easy to work with and made writing a book for my practice very easy. Their services have helped to separate my business from our competitors. I highly recommend Joe Preston and Phil Guye and their firm DoctorBookPublishing.com."
-Dr. Mark F. Hardison, DDS

"First thing I want to say about Joe and Phil is that they are very - I want to use the word as a doctor would say patient-centered. But they are very client-centered. I think that what we lack is the ability to put ourselves in our patients' shoes. Joe and Phil frame and position you and they do the framing of the marketing before the patient even arrives in your office."

-Dr. Coury Staadecker, DDS, MS

"One of my biggest concerns before hiring someone to do my SEO number one is that they would be knowledgeable and number two is that they would be able to really deliver the goods and get me on the top of page one and Joe Preston and Phil Guye couldn't be better in both categories. Joe and Phil are virtually the encyclopedia of SEO knowledge and they are always keeping themselves current. And I use them as a resource too because I enjoy SEO myself and I like calling them and bouncing marketing ideas off them or picking their brains. And ever since they have been on my team I've been number one on Google search for all my keywords and that's a real boost for my practice. So, I appreciate the work Joe and Phil have done for me and I really couldn't recommend them more highly."

-Dr. David Scharf, DMD

"Joe Preston and Phil Guye really have an interesting perspective. We are not our customer. We are not our patients. Joe and Phil come with an incredible perspective, a different perspective. They see things the way the patient sees it. And that speaks about them for what they are capable of doing for us. That's just an incredible, incredible insight into our patients' mind and how is it that we're going to target that patient. What's going to make that patient come to us when they don't even know us. We're on the right track with Joe and Phil and their company."

-Dr. Ed De Endrade, DDS

"Joe, Phil and their staff streamline a potentially time-consuming, difficult and tedious process thereby making it extremely efficient and manageable. The vision and marketing prowess of Mr. Preston and Mr. Guye comes alive in the book writing process making it a pleasure to work with them."

-Dr. Jason Stoner, DDS, MS

A NOTE FOR OUR READERS

We wrote this book for our clients that we
are honored to serve and help each day.
We are blessed to work with some of the
most successful doctors and surgeons
in the world.

Our goal for this book was to capture some
of our best influence and persuasion strategies and provide you with what we call
The Secret Recipe To Grow Referrals.

Enjoy Our Recipe!

For media inquiries or additional information on our marketing solutions including book publishing, best seller book marketing campaigns, online reputation management, SEO, public relations, patient indoctrination videos, cinematic storytelling, online advertising campaigns and advanced influence and persuasion strategies, please contact:

Phillip Guye & Joseph Preston

DoctorBookPublishing.com
An Imprint of Deep Think Media

3480 Barham Boulevard
Suite 322
Hollywood Hills, CA 90068 USA
1-323-851-3825

1425 K Street, NW
Suite 350
Washington, DC 20005 USA
1-800-704-3447

media@DoctorBookPublishing.com

If you represent an association, academic institution or other organization, we offer quantity discounts on bulk purchases of this book or any of our other books. Please call 1-800-704-3447 or email sales@DoctorBookPublishing.com.

TABLE OF CONTENTS

Introduction:
Are You Taking Business For Granted? 27
  Introducing The Winning Strategy 29
  Snooze You Lose 33

The Goal:
Achieving A Bulletproof Reputation 43
  A Recognized Expert 45
  Be The Authority 51
  Making A Name 61

The Solution:
Author = Authority 67
  One Book - Endless Benefits 69
  Two's Company -
  Three's Good Business Sense 91

Don't Scrimp - Choose Hardcover 101
More Ways To Leverage Your Book 111

The Plan:
From Strategy To Publication 129
   Bring The Pain 131
   Make It Personal 139
   Doing It Right As A Diyer 147
   Doing It Wrong As A Diyer 157

The Short Cut:
The 5 Hour Solution 167
   The Pain Free Version 169
   Five Hours! 175
   Quality Control 183
   One Book = Many Books 189

The Bottom Line:
He Who Hesitates 197
   One More Thing 199

About The Co-Authors 215

www.PlasticSurgeonMarketingMotto.com

"Sorry Randolph! The Yellow Pages is just not building my plastic surgery practice anymore. We need to cut the cord."

Scan this QR Code to share with colleagues.

INTRODUCTION:

ARE YOU TAKING BUSINESS FOR GRANTED?

www.PlasticSurgeonMarketingMotto.com

"Can you tell me exactly where my plastic surgery website will be positioned on Google next week? Page one, two, three, four, five, six, seven..."

INTRODUCING THE WINNING STRATEGY

H OW'S BUSINESS?
That can be a tricky question to answer. Sure, you might be able to say that, right now, things are good and you have a steady stream of patients, but you no doubt recognize that the true measure of a practice is not what it's doing now but, rather, what it's projected to do over the next few years.

And when your practice is dependent on a regular influx of new patients, you can't afford to take anything for granted.

A bad review online could turn prospects away. Long-time allies could start sending their referrals to other plastic surgeons or cosmetic surgeons.

Or a competing surgeon or practice could develop

a winning marketing strategy that interrupts your flow of new patients.

It doesn't matter whether your practice is struggling, ticking along nicely, or booming; if you don't have a cutting-edge marketing strategy in place to move your business forward and keep it ahead of the competition, it's only a matter of time before you find yourself playing catch up.

There are, of course, many different marketing strategies that you could employ. But, in our experience, a symbiotic strategy performed really well will always defeat someone who dabbles in lots of different tactics that are executed half heartedly.

And the powerful strategy we're going to reveal in this book is going to blow all of your competition away.

We're talking about putting you so far ahead of the pack that it's unlikely anyone will ever be able to get near you.

Ok, so there's no point tiptoeing around it. You've read the book description, skimmed the contents page and maybe even skipped ahead a little bit. It's no secret that the marketing strategy we're going to lay down in these pages is built around the concept of transforming you into a published author.

We understand that this may seem like a bold

choice of marketing. You may also be wondering how you're expected to find the time to write a book in the first place.

Well, first of all, this book is going to teach you how to become a published author in as little as five hours of your valuable time. So please put the time-restraints concern out of your head for now. Seriously, it's not an issue.

And as for using a book as a marketing vehicle... We're going to get into this in a lot more detail but if you have any doubts about this concept, your concerns will disappear in just a few chapters. You're not going to believe the ripple effects that can come from this one, simple strategy.

But if you're struggling to contain your cynicism, consider this...

This marketing strategy is so powerful that we're using it ourselves. And the fact that you're reading this book means that it's already working.

You see, this book doesn't just teach this marketing strategy.

It's also a physical example of the strategy in action.

Let that thought sit for a moment or two and then read on.

www.PlasticSurgeonMarketingMotto.com

"I got a great idea...in addition to selling to plastic surgeons and cosmetic surgeons, let's sell our BOTOX® products to cosmetic dentists and really expand our market."

Scan this QR Code to share with colleagues.

SNOOZE YOU LOSE

HIGH ON THE LIST OF things people rarely say is the phrase:

"I really enjoyed having invasive surgery."

Or perhaps... "I certainly look forward to having difficulty breathing from my nose as I recover from rhinoplasty."

How about this one: "I love going to the doctor!"

Sorry people. We know you take great care to make every one of your patients as comfortable as possible in Spa-like environments, but the fact remains that, for most people, a trip to the plastic surgeon can be filled with great anxiety and fear.

Even the patient that has nothing more than a quick post-op follow-up appointment and a clean bill of health has to go through the trepidation of wondering what the doctor might find and the vulnerability that comes from having to disrobe in a medical office.

A growing challenge for the plastic surgery profession is that doctor referrals (doctor to specialist) and patient-to-patient recommendations are more difficult to generate.

Someone who enjoys a fine meal at a restaurant will happily tell everyone about it, but a successful trip to the plastic surgeon isn't always likely to become a topic of conversation. It doesn't matter how pain free the procedure, how professional the doctor or how beautifully decorated the office, it just isn't that likely to be talked about outside of close family and best of friends. The patient-to-patient referral phenomenon is dependent on the personality of the patient and how candid they are about sharing personal health matters.

Even the best visit to the doctor is still an event that most people would prefer to put out of their minds until their next appointment.

That isn't to say that referrals don't happen; they happen all the time. Let us put it this way. If you don't own a $5 million practice, you could be busier. You could have more patients. On the other hand, if you don't own a $10 million practice, you could be busier. You could have more patients. They are out there.

When someone is looking for a plastic or cosmetic surgeon, they may well ask their friends and family for a recommendation. Referrals are just harder to come by.

Which makes it all the more important that your practice is primed to encourage referrals at every possible opportunity. You may not think it to be so but it **IS** possible to influence and persuade people to the point where they feel encouraged or even obliged to tell other people about your practice.

And in marketing terms, referrals are the golden ticket. The "endorsed introduction" is the number one marketing tactic...ever. Period. The end.

No amount of branding exercises, clever slogans and special offers can compete with a trusted friend or family member saying "my plastic surgeon is really good, I highly recommend him or her."

In marketing speak, our firm refers to this as a form of "Social Proof." When people want help with a purchasing decision, it's an easy shortcut to ask a friend for a recommendation because the thinking is that "if my friend likes this doctor's service and results, I'll probably like them as well."

This also holds true if you are a plastic surgeon and many of your referrals come from family doctors, internists, dermatologists, breast cancer surgeons or ob-gyns. When these docs refer their patients to you, those referrals can have at least as much power as a friend's recommendation because the doctors are positioned as authorities and their opinions are considered to be of very high value. However, most doctors will recommend two or sometimes three surgeons and let the patient decide who to select. Unfortunately, this is for legal reasons so the doctors avoid potential lawsuits from mentally disturbed and disgruntled patients.

Even if a doctor isn't giving you a specific seal of approval, the simple act of suggesting your practice IMPLIES that, at least on some level, an endorsement is being made.

You're probably already well aware that referrals are more inclined to accept treatment and easier to convert into paying customers than leads from any other source. In fact, it's not too much of a stretch to suggest that the health of your practice, both now and in the future, is going to depend greatly on the volume of referrals you receive. Unless, of course, you embrace the direct marketing model and invest significant capital into TV ads, radio ads, billboards, newspaper ads, PR, direct mail and Internet marketing.

Can publishing a book increase the number of referrals you receive? The short answer is yes.

We'll address that in depth soon but, for now, we just want you to be clear in your mind that generating MORE referrals should be the primary goal of your marketing efforts.

And this being the case, the longer you delay in taking action in this regard, the more likely you are to lose out. Right now, whether you're aware of it or not, you are facing two significant threats to your business.

1. Losing Your Patient Supply

If you're taking the time to consider your business and marketing strategy, you can be sure that some if not all of your competition is also doing the same. So what will happen if one of your competitors comes up with a creative, yet ethical incentive strategy that results in referrals being directed towards them... and away from you?

This is of particular concern if you're specializing in blepharoplasty, brow lifts, cheek augmentations, chin surgery, face lifts, forehead lifts, neck lifts, otoplasty, abdominoplasty, arm lifts, breast augmentations, breast reconstructions, breast reductions, labiaplasty, liposuctions or tummy tucks. Most likely, your business primarily depends on referrals from other doctors and patients. All the more so if the majority of your referrals come from a hand full of sources.

It's all well and good to consider how you can increase the number of referrals you receive and the number of avenues from which you receive them, but you also need to give serious attention to SECURING the flow of referrals that you already enjoy.

Yes, you may be thinking, but I have a great relationship with this particular doctor and he or she's been sending me referrals for years. This really doesn't apply to me.

You're fooling yourself. That's like assuming your marriage is solid and thinking you can take your spouse for granted. Relationships, personal and business, don't last forever unless you keep working on them. Neglect them and they'll fall apart faster than you can blink.

How long can your business survive if your existing flow of referrals suddenly dries up because one of your competitors acts quickly and freezes you out? Once this happens it can be very difficult to reverse.

SNOOZE YOU LOSE

2. Competing With The Grays.

Every industry has a sizeable gray area that sits between what is legal and what is ethical.

I'm sure you don't need us to convince you that operating in the gray is a hazardous short-term strategy that will eventually catch up with you. But that isn't the problem here.

The problem is OTHER surgeons operating in the gray area and, as a result, sucking patients away from you. It doesn't matter if the other guy eventually gets a bad rep and goes out of business because he's hurting you right now.

The satisfaction of seeing the other guy go out of business is going to be a bitter pill if you go out of business right alongside him because he killed your cash flow.

One of the things we're increasingly seeing is a "bait and switch" tactic where doctors advertise a medical procedure for a ridiculously low price, simply to get the customer into the office. Our marketing firm refers to this as Garage Sale Medicine and Yard Sale Surgery.

Once they've lured people in, they actually discourage one type of procedure by placing Fear, Uncertainty and Doubt (the FUD factor) in the minds of the prospective patients. These unethical grays may talk about the length of time it takes to recover from the procedure and convince them, instead, to opt for an inferior solution. The patient should leave in disgust, and some do, but many are too embarrassed to complain.

Yes, it's deeply unethical, but it's also highly effective at steering people AWAY from your office. That's tough to compete with.

That's one example. We could also talk about some doctors who are treating patients despite only completing a short training course in a specific procedure.

Of course, the patient is better off seeing a specialist who has performed hundreds or thousands of surgeries and has completed an extensive residency but, if they never visit your office, how are you ever going to get a chance to explain the difference? And the words "board certified" may be significant to you, but the average person has no idea what this means exactly.

This is what you're up against. If you're not already feeling the squeeze from the competition, unethical or otherwise, it's only a matter of time before you do.

If it's certain that you cannot afford to do nothing, it's equally certain that you can't afford to delay.

You must choose an effective marketing strategy

now and implement it as if your business depends on it.

Because, in all likelihood, it does.

www.PlasticSurgeonMarketingMotto.com

"I need to refer my patient to a plastic surgeon for a beak job."

Scan this QR Code to share with colleagues.

THE GOAL:

TRUST & CREDIBILITY - ACHIEVING
A BULLETPROOF REPUTATION

www.PlasticSurgeonMarketingMotto.com

"Bill, do you think this strategy for acquiring new patients is a little outdated?"

Scan this QR Code to share with colleagues.

A RECOGNIZED EXPERT

T RUST AND CREDIBILITY ARE TRICKY things because it often takes time to establish these credentials. If you treat a patient successfully for many years, these qualities will shine through to that individual. But, when you're trying to attract new patients, you don't have that kind of time.

You need to be able to exude trust and credibility, almost instantly, while a potential patient is still weighing options.

No small feat. But if you can do it, you can become virtually bulletproof in your marketplace.

You will become the natural choice for referrals. You can easily justify premium pricing, and even the occasional negative comment or review online won't be able to counteract the power of the reputation you've established. By the way, everyone can get a bad review. There are crazy and unreasonable patients out there... not to mention the disgruntled former employees that you recently fired!

During this chapter, and the next two, we will consider three core ways in which you can establish trust and credibility. Starting with...

ESTABLISHING YOURSELF AS AN EXPERT.

The first thing you need to be aware of is that there's no minimum level of knowledge and ability required before someone becomes an expert.

In fact, one synonym for the word "expert" is "proficient." Hardly inspiring. By that standard, everyone is an expert in something, even if it's just watching football and eating Cheetos.

And it's all relative.

Put a high school science teacher next to Albert Einstein and, although you can say that they're both experts in the subject of science, most people would consider the latter to be the "true" expert.

So, yes, you're already an expert. Your MD degree, your countless hours of continuing education and your experience establish this to be true. But, to build a heightened reputation in your field that is founded on trust and credibility, you need to go further. You need to become the "recognized" expert to avoid being an "invisible" expert.

This is the point at which you no longer need to tell people you're an expert because it's evident by what you've achieved and, crucially, because other influencers such as the news media are proclaiming you to be such.

When you're a recognized expert you become, at least in your part of the world, the voice for your profession to the outside world. You're the person that local and national television new shows, radio shows, newspapers, and magazines go to when they want an expert opinion on a plastic surgery or aesthetics topic.

This isn't about ego, or loving the spotlight. It's about something bigger than you: it's about sharing your message and helping as many people achieve total health and wellness along with improved self-confidence and peace of mind. You must embrace your role as the messenger (also known as the marketer).

Other doctors will be confidently proud to refer their patients to you because being able to place their patients in front of a recognized expert makes them look good by association.

And if your position as a recognized expert is strong enough, you don't even need to say it. Your reputation will precede you and your trust and credibility will be assumed.

How do you make the transition from "expert" to "recognized expert?"

You need to start a chain reaction. Take the right steps to position yourself as an expert now and, in time, one or two influencers will start to refer to you as THE expert. Next, others will add their voice to the claim. And before long the movement will take on a life of its own and your expert moniker is assured…

Along with your trust and credibility.

www.PlasticSurgeonMarketingMotto.com

"I am glad to hear you want to follow in my foot steps and become a plastic surgeon when you grow up. Here is my only advice...also study marketing, sales, influence, persuasion, PR, SEO, conversion strategies..."

Scan this QR Code to share with colleagues.

BE THE AUTHORITY

B ETWEEN THE TWO AUTHORS OF this book, we
have more than 40 years experience in marketing,
advertising, cinematic storytelling and public relations.
Here's our combined bio:

*Phillip Guye and Joseph Preston are Senior Manag-
ing Partners of Doctor Reputation Management (www.
DrReputationManagement.com), a leading marketing
solutions firm they co-founded to provide their clients with
the highest level of patient and customer acquisition success currently available in the marketplace.*

*By leveraging the skills and techniques they creat-
ed and enhanced over 22 years for intensive reputation
management, public relations, advanced search engine
optimization (SEO) and viral video marketing, Preston,
Guye and their team help many of the nation's leading*

doctors, medical practices and hospitals. Their proprietary "Patient-Getting" formula for creating Patient Indoctrination Videos positively influences prospective patients so that they truly get to Know, Like, Trust and Fall In Love with doctors and their practices before the initial consultation. Phil and Joe are also the co-founders of Doctor Book Publishing, a multi-channel media publishing company dedicated to transforming leading doctors into published authors and media celebrities.

Phillip Guye has helped companies such as Boeing, Warner Bros., ABC, Nissan, Levi's, Hot Topic, Mercedes Benz, Funny Or Die and College Humor. Utilizing a variety of marketing disciplines, Phil Guye has also worked with celebrities and artists including: 50 Cent, Snoop Dog, Dr. Dre, Rihanna, Pamela Anderson, Ice Cube, Roy Disney, Rip Torn and George Clooney. He oversees the Los Angeles office as well as the firm's green screen and white cyc film studio.

Guye's unique understanding of how to influence prospects to become customers and persuade them to virally endorse these products via social media has created a demand from pharmaceutical companies and sporting goods manufacturers for his strategic counsel on everything from brand positioning to package design as well as new worldwide product launches.

Phillip Guye, a bonafide authority and recognized expert on search engine optimization, has been hired by SEO software companies for his insight on advanced product development and feature enhancements.

Featured in Forbes magazine, Vanity Fair magazine, Time magazine, USA Today, BusinessWeek Small Biz magazine as well as interviewed on CNN and Fox News, Joseph Preston has helped companies ranging in size from start-ups to the Fortune 500 including The Home Depot, McDonalds, Reebok, Playtex and RedBox.

According to a feature article in Forbes magazine, "Joseph Preston worked a crowd of reporters who gathered at Washington, D.C.'s posh Galileo restaurant and then rushed off to their newsrooms to give Preston airtime... Preston, who has been in public relations since he was 19, managed to plant a story on the cover of USA Today's Life section...Within two days images of Preston aired on the national news and on some 30 local stations...The Sunday Times of London, Time magazine and other print media ran with the story."

As a reputation and PR strategist overseeing the Washington, DC office, Preston has successfully influenced and persuaded journalists from a variety of national media outlets to interview and feature his clientele in The Wall Street Journal, New York Times, Washington Post, Los Angeles Times, Newsweek, Glamour, Elle, InStyle, New York Post, New York Daily News, Associated Press, CBS, ABC, NBC and the Huffington Post. To prepare his clients for media interviews and crisis situations, Joseph Preston conducts intensive media training for CEOs, doctors, attorneys and spokespersons of both large and small organizations.

As a passionate and engaging speaker, Mr. Preston has lectured and presented internationally at various medical, university and corporate events on topics including: patient/customer acquisition strategies, reputation management, public relations, SEO, book publishing, book marketing, patient indoctrination videos and cinematic storytelling.

Both Phil's and Joe's unique understanding of the Google algorithm, Google's ever evolving updates and other second tier search engine sensitivities has enabled them to co-author other books including Green Eggs And Google For Kids, Green Eggs And Google: SEO for the CEO and Reputation Management 911: Defuse Online Attackers & Disarm Dishonest Competitors. Guye and Preston are also the co-authors of four medical marketing books including: Dental Marketing Motto, Doctor Marketing Motto, Orthopedic Surgeon Marketing Motto and Plastic Surgeon Marketing Motto.

During our professional careers, the finest written work on the subject of marketing that we've ever come across is Robert Cialdini's book entitled Influence: The Psychology of Persuasion.

If you read one other book, on the subject of marketing, make sure it's that one.

Sound interesting?

Think on that for a moment.

Experience tells us that, out of everyone who reads the above paragraphs, some will store that information away and may purchase the book if they stumble across it while browsing Amazon, some will make a mental note to check the book out next time they're online, some will add "buy this book" to their "to do" list, and others won't have read this paragraph yet because they're already on Amazon, credit card in hand.

Significantly, almost no one will completely ignore or dismiss the advice to buy this book.

Why? We've told you almost nothing about the book other than that we think it's great (and it really is). But for most readers this will be enough to make them seriously consider making the purchase.

Whether or not the reader follows through and actually buys the book is irrelevant for the purposes of this discussion; what's important is that our casual recommendation is enough to stir interest.

The reason for this is down to the power of "authority." As human beings, when we perceive someone to be in a position of responsibility or to be in possession of important knowledge that we don't have, we view them, to at least some degree, as an authority.

And that status inclines us to take greater notice of their suggestions and recommendations.

Robert Cialdini's aforementioned book covers this subject in depth but, suffice to say, the greater your perceived level of authority, the greater influence you have over people's opinions and decisions.

In this instance, the fact that we've collectively spent around four decades working in marketing and, perhaps more significantly, have written books on the subject, gives us a level of authority status in this field. So, when we recommend a book on the subject of marketing, at the very least you're likely to have assumed that, if you want to learn more on the subject, this book is going to be a worthwhile purchase.

BE THE AUTHORITY

As a qualified medical practitioner you also have a healthy measure of authority. The act of putting the title "Dr." before your name or MD after your name only adds to this. At its most basic level this means that, if a layperson wants an opinion on what treatment to obtain, your view is going to carry more weight than that of an average person.

Here's the problem…

Every surgeon, or doctor, is viewed as a medical authority.

And if everyone is an authority…then no one is an authority.

If your prospective patients (also known as prospective customers) view every surgeon on the same level, this advantage is lost and they're going to default to going with the doctor that a friend recommends or that "bait and switch" guy who is a ferocious advertiser and offers such great prices.

So, here's what you're going to do. You're going to stop being just AN authority, and you're going to…

TURN YOURSELF INTO THE AUTHORITY.

If you set yourself even just a couple of steps above everyone else, you stand apart and the power of authority comes back into play along with its ability to influence people's decisions and opinions.

And here's a bonus. If you specialize in a certain area of plastic surgery and become the recognized authority in that particular field, you also become the easy choice for doctors who want to refer their patients to the best plastic surgeon in the local market.

Becoming an authority takes a little effort but probably not as much as you think. In fact, in this chapter alone, we've already hinted at two relatively simple ways to accomplish this.

Don't worry if you missed them. All will be revealed shortly.

www.PlasticSurgeonMarketingMotto.com

"Doc, he needs a tummy tuck so bad the cat wanted to take a nap in his big soft belly."

Scan this QR Code to share with colleagues.

MAKING A NAME

B ECOMING A CELEBRITY HAS NEVER been easier.

Talent, ability and knowledge are completely superfluous when it's sufficient to act outrageously on a reality TV show.

In a world where you can forge a career in being enduringly famous simply for being momentarily famous, it's no wonder that more and more people see it as a short-cut to "success."

Relax, we're not about to suggest that you audition for the Voice or America's Got Talent. Or do anything that you would consider demeaning or damaging to your reputation as a professional.

However, we are going to advise that, at least on a local level, you consider the benefits of...

DEVELOPING CELEBRITY STATUS.

You transformed into a celebrity plastic surgeon? Really?

Absolutely. Control your incredulity for a moment. And control, also, your distaste for the idea. We're not talking about becoming some kind of pathetic attention-seeker. And we're definitely not talking about seeking fame for its own sake. We're talking about a controlled effort to raise the profile of your name and, in the process, attach more credibility to it.

As much as we may have come to look down on the culture of celebrity, the fact remains that the majority of people still desire an elevated status and have respect for those that have achieved it. Even if it's only recognized within one specific field and in one particular geographical area.

And YOUR celebrity status isn't going to be built on notoriety; it's going to be founded on your expertise in your work in plastic surgery and enhancing people's mental and physical lives.

For an example of the power of celebrity, consider the employment law firm that has built a sizeable, national client base and has achieved this with virtually no traditional advertising. The majority of the firm's most lucrative clients come from one source...

The CEO writes a weekly column for a national newspaper.

Although it might not seem like it, this individual has become, by definition, a celebrity. In his own particular field and within his target market, his name and company has a higher profile than the competition.

And by "competition" I mean all those companies who are desperately trying to keep up.

This is the kind of celebrity status we're talking about. Television appearances, newspaper columns, radio talk shows and magazine interviews. The power of the media will raise your credibility to a level you can't even begin to appreciate until it happens.

This creates two benefits. On the one hand, some of the people who witness your celebrity appearances will be impressed and want to become your patients. And those who don't see it will be impressed to learn of it when they see the recordings on your website and the framed articles on your office waiting room walls.

We already discussed briefly that media appearances help to establish your expertise but, in many ways, the celebrity status is even more beneficial. For some of your patients, just being treated by a local celebrity will make their day. Others will get a kick of being able to boast that their doctor was interviewed on their favorite morning TV show.

Your patients may not talk to their friends about the chin surgery they just endured. But they will be only too pleased to brag that they were treated by that doctor who was interviewed on ABC, CBS, CNN, FOX, NBC or written about in the local newspaper.

We absolutely love this marketing approach because, in virtually every industry, most of the players don't have the PR savvy or guts to step up and do this. They'll prevaricate by saying it's "beneath them" or that they're "too busy," but really they just lack confidence in their media savvy or expertise.

You're smarter than that. And, if you take the plunge when no one else has the courage, you'll own your market. No one will be able to match the marketing power of this strategy.

Expertise, authority, and celebrity status are, individually, highly effective tools for establishing your trust and credibility, and solidifying your place in the market.

But combine them and you become unstoppable. You become untouchable. You become bulletproof. And you'll be even more pleased to hear...

You can tackle all three goals at once with just one simple solution.

Turn the page to get started.

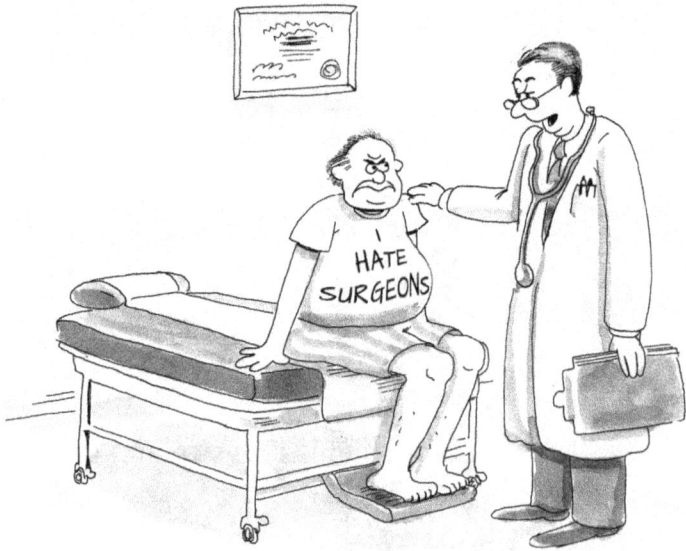

www.PlasticSurgeonMarketingMotto.com

"I'm happy to see you too. Obviously, you have not read
my Amazon #1 best selling book on plastic surgery."

Scan this QR Code to share with colleagues.

THE SOLUTION:

AUTHOR = AUTHORITY

www.PlasticSurgeonMarketingMotto.com

"Is the list of happy patients who have NOT left an online review ready yet?"

Scan this QR Code to share with colleagues.

ONE BOOK - ENDLESS BENEFITS

I T'S SAID THAT EVERYONE HAS at least one book in them.

Most people believe this to be true. Maybe we have expertise we'd love to share. Perhaps our life story would make a riveting bestseller. Or, most commonly, we have a great idea for a novel that we're convinced no one else has ever thought up.

So, why is it that so few people ever actually get down to business and write something?

Because it's hard.

Putting pen to paper (or these days, fingers to keyboard) for easily in excess of 200 hours is a considerable undertaking. And that's even assuming you have the ability to write smooth, enjoyable prose.

The difference between having something worth

writing and having the ability and focus to sit down and get the job done is a chasm of Grand Canyon proportions.

Which is why when someone actually does write a book we can't help but be a little bit in awe.

Technology has made it faster and simpler to shoot movies, build websites, take on DIY projects and so on. But writing a book? That's still 99% down to the ability of the writer. Just like composing music and painting beautiful landscapes, we recognize it as an art and a considerable achievement.

You can even take finding a New York publisher and hitting the New York Times bestseller lists out of the equation. Simply writing a book is enough to earn respect. John Grisham said that after writing *A Time to Kill* he always figured that even if he never found a publisher he could still keep the manuscript in his office and use it to impress people.

This is why you're going to love being an author and why, if handled correctly, it will turn out to be the best thing that ever happened to your practice.

In this section we're going to dig into the strategy and engage in a comprehensive consideration of all the different ways you can leverage publishing a book to strengthen and develop your practice. Even if, at this point, you feel you've already got a good idea of how this is going to play out, you're going to be amazed at just how much you can leverage the single act of publishing a book.

We'll start by considering six key benefits of becoming a published author.

Benefit #1 – Trust And Credibility

Unless you are J.K. Rowling of Harry Potter fame, you're not going to get rich on royalties selling your book. Your plastic surgery book will not likely hit the New York Times bestseller list (although you can hit an incredibly significant bestseller list in specific categories – more on this later).

The reason for this is because the subject of your book is going to target a very narrow audience. But, crucially, almost 100% of this target audience will be made up of people who are either the prospective patients you're aiming to attract and influence or members of the news media. And the rest of the audience will consist of doctors who can help send even more referrals your way.

When someone reads your book, learns how to

take proper action to enhance their beauty as well as restore their mental health, and feels better about you and the outcome you can deliver, then, at that particular moment in that person's life, you are a celebrity, an expert, and an authority all rolled into one. The credibility you've just gained is immense.

Even if someone only reads part of your book, or even just picks up the book and skims the text on the front and back, you'll be recognized as an author, and your credibility in your chosen field will rise.

Guaranteed.

Let's face it...writing a book is the ultimate symbol of authority in our culture. A book creates INSTANT AUTHORITY.

Generating trust and credibility is only one of the benefits of publishing a book. But, as we considered in the previous section, it's incredibly powerful and is arguably the key reason why you should adopt this strategy.

In almost every industry, most businesses base their marketing decisions on what the competition is doing. Business A advertises in this magazine so I will too.

Business B advertises on Google Adwords so I'd better get in there as well.

The problem with this approach is that, if you only do what everyone else does, standing out from the crowd becomes incredibly difficult.

But how many plastic surgeons and cosmetic surgeons are actually going to invest their time and energy into writing and publishing a book?

At the time of writing, if you go to Amazon.com and search for books on plastic surgery you'll find a number of clinical books aimed at practitioners and only a couple of books aimed at consumers. There is a HUGE opportunity here to separate yourself from the competition; to draw a line in the sand that says: "Yes, there are lots of specialists in this field, but I'm THE authority because I'm the surgeon that wrote the book on the subject."

Give 100 patients the choice between two plastic surgeons and tell them that their training, facilities and prices are more or less the same. But, by the way, Dr. Y wrote a book on the subject.

Who is going to "close" the most patients and obtain the highest case acceptance?

The prospective patients don't even have to read the

book. The published author, by implication, is going to have more credibility, more authority... and ultimately more patients.

Benefit #2 – Professional Praise

The credibility that comes with publishing a book is not solely reserved for consumers, it also extends to your fellow professionals.

Again, even if they never read the book, the simple fact that you've published one will earn you respect. Not least because they'll be wondering how you managed to find the time to operate a busy practice AND write a book (we'll show you later on how to do this without the massive time investment).

You might not be wild about the idea of public speaking but, if you can handle it, your book can open the door to joining the speaking circuit. Study clubs, professional associations, even companies that sell medical equipment, are always on the lookout for people to speak at their events. Being able to present yourself as a published author will make you a credible choice. In fact, being able to present yourself as a #1 Best Selling author will make you THE only choice.

Listen to this introduction: "I'm very pleased now

to invite to the stage Dr. Jason Stoner, Columbus Ohio board certified periodontist and author of the five time Amazon #1 best selling book entitled LANAP Laser Gum Surgery."

Our publishing company DoctorBookPublishing.com helped board certified periodontist Dr. Jason Stoner publish, ghostwrite, edit, design, print and market two leading medical books entitled: LANAP Laser Gum Surgery and Dental Implants Columbus. In fact, we helped Dr. Stoner's LANAP book achieve best seller status in five categories on Amazon including: #1 Best Seller in Oral Surgery Books, #1 Best Seller in Periodontics Books, #1 Best Seller in Dentistry Kindle eBooks, #1 Best Seller in Oral Surgery Kindle eBooks and #1 Best Seller in Periodontics Kindle eBooks. We have the Amazon best seller list screen shots to prove it.

Let's face it...books do not become best sellers on their own. A marketing campaign for your book needs to be executed.

It doesn't matter that the book was not the best seller that beat out fiction writers John Grisham, James Patterson or J.K. Rowling on Amazon.com and it doesn't matter that your publisher is not Simon and Schuster. Because how many other people in your field of expertise, in your city (or even your state), have gone to the trouble of writing and publishing a book?

Two? One? Probably no one.

You stepped up so you're the one reaping the rewards.

And although we don't want to get too far ahead of ourselves here, every event at which you speak, every association you join, and every study club you chair is another endorsement that can be featured in the "About The Author" section of the second edition of your book!

Benefit #3 – Patient Acquisition

Patient acquisition is about closing the deal. When you convince a patient to accept a particular treatment or commit to surgery you're adding something to your bottom line. But first you've got to close the deal and achieve agreement from the patient to proceed with treatment and pay for your solution.

We'll consider in more detail later on how a book can increase the number of referrals you receive, but can it also increase your rate of case acceptance?

The answer, in almost every case, is yes.

Remember, a key effect of producing a book is a

healthy dose of trust and credibility. This means that, in the past, all the prospective patients who consulted with you, who were on the fence, but who ultimately did not accept treatment, might have swung the other way if they knew you to be a published author.

It's not going to push everyone over the edge but, if you track all your numbers, this strategy will produce a measurable difference and advantage.

And this is only the residual effect. Imagine for a minute that you're advising a patient on the virtues of breast augmentation. The patient is hesitant so you offer them a complimentary copy of your breast augmentation book, and arrange for your patient coordinator to follow-up with them next week.

You don't have to be a marketing expert to understand how powerful this is.

The book will answer all their questions, allay all of their fears, and, I know we keep saying it, but even if they don't read all or EVEN ANY of the book, the implied authority and expertise that comes with having written a book on the subject (not to mention the gratitude you've generated by giving them a free book with a retail value of $26 as a gift) is going to have an impact.

It's not a panacea. It's not going to increase your

conversion rate to 100%. But it's almost impossible for it not to have an incremental positive effect.

You may find it helpful to sit down and crunch some numbers. Look at your records and calculate how many prospects you converted into patients during the last 12 months. Then total up the gross profit from all of those procedures. Divide the second number by the first to get your average gross profit per customer.

Now work out what would happen to your bottom line if publishing a book improved your case acceptance by 1%. What about 2%? Or 3%? Just imagine 10%...or even 20%.

These are conservative numbers, and there's no reason why you shouldn't see a much greater effect, but even this small increase can make a massive difference to your overall profits.

And this is just the primary effect. Some of those additional patients that you convert will become consistent patients for years to come. Some of them will bring in referrals by talking to friends and family.

Publishing a book is a short-term and long- term strategy all rolled into one. And remember, an increase in case acceptance is just one residual benefit among many.

Benefit #4 – Capturing Online Leads

When looking for a surgeon for a specific treatment, many still turn to their family doctor, internist or dermatologist for advice. These days, though, it's becoming more common for people to start with Google. However, an even more recent trend has seen people turning to Amazon for guidance.

The reason for this is that it's getting harder and harder to find reliable advice online, especially if the subject is a profitable one. Articles and blogs pop up here, there, and everywhere, sometimes with conflicting information and often with a clear agenda to push a particular product or service.

When people don't trust the information they find on random websites such as Yahoo Answers or Yelp, they turn to the providers they trust, one of which is Amazon...for their books. Everybody loves shortcuts. And these days the fastest way to find reliable and in-depth information on just about any subject is to find a book on the subject, especially if the information can be quickly downloaded to a Kindle, lap top, tablet or smartphone. While Google is the #1 **information** search engine in the world with more than 17 billion searches conducted each month in the US, Amazon has evolved into the #1 **buying** search engine in the world with more than $61 billion in annual revenues.

It's not an entirely unreasonable assumption to believe that an author who has taken the time and trouble to publish a book on a subject is more likely to have expended effort on research and accuracy and, as a consequence, have more credibility than someone who's thrown up a couple of articles alongside a bunch of ads. Little wonder that this market is growing rapidly.

At the time of writing…

Amazon has more than 200 million credit cards on file (so their customers can make easy one click purchases).

The Kindle Reader software is available for the Mac, PC, Android phones and tablets, iPhone and iPad.

For every 100 hardback and paperback books sold on Amazon, customers download 114 Kindle eBooks.

By publishing your book through Amazon (in both physical and digital formats), you gain access to a blossoming market that, at least for now, is massively underserved in plastic surgery-related health subjects for consumers.

Couple this with the fact that you can tailor your book for your region or town by calling it, for example, "Dental Implants Nashville and Murfreesboro" or "Dental Implants Columbus" and you have a real window of opportunity to put yourself in front of a highly targeted audience.

Our publishing company (DoctorBookPub- lishing.com) helped board certified oral surgeon Dr. Mark Hardison publish, ghostwrite, edit, design, print and market his book Dental Implants Nashville and Murfreesboro. We also helped Dr. Hardison achieve best seller status in three categories on Amazon including: #1 Best Seller in Oral Surgery Books, #1 Best Seller in Dentistry Kindle eBooks and #1 Best Seller in Oral Surgery Kindle eBooks.

Benefit #5 – Answer Awkward Questions

People are apprehensive about surgical procedures for lots of reasons.

But mostly it's about pain, scarring and fear of surgical failure.

Is this procedure and healing process going to hurt and, if so, by how much on a scale that runs from mildly uncomfortable to so excruciating I want to pull out my own toe nails to distract myself?

And yet you may not get asked these types of questions all the time. Why? Maybe because it feels rude to ask a surgeon, in effect, "are you going to hurt me or scar me forever?" Or perhaps it's just because people don't want to sound weak or childish. Particularly male patients.

There are few men who can say "is this going to hurt?" without feeling ever so slightly emasculated.

And this problem is more keenly observed when the patient is male and the surgeon is female.

There, we said it. It might be sexist but it's also true.

This is where a book is a lifeline. Your patients may not be keen to discuss their most pressing psychological fears, even if you broach the subject first, but if you give them your book to take home that answers these questions (as opposed to a flimsy pamphlet or a mass produced brochure that resides in all your competitors' offices), you get over this hurdle without making the person feel awkward or uncomfortable.

A smart approach is to add a "Frequently Asked Questions" and "Should Ask Questions" section to your book covering the most critical questions or the most awkward and uncomfortable questions. Point this section out when you give the prospective patient your book so that, even if they don't read the whole thing, they can still find the section that matters most to them, leaving them more inclined to commit to the surgery.

Benefit #6 – Neuters Bad Reviews

It's a well-established fact that someone is far more likely to go to the trouble of visiting a website and writing a review if they've had a bad experience than if they had a good one. Unfortunately, you're occasionally going to come across an unreasonable or mentally unstable patient who may actually be from another planet or even galaxy. It may or may not be your fault. Maybe there were circumstances out of your control. Perhaps the referring doctor gave the patient unrealistic expectations. In fact, it's quite possible that the patient was just a bit of a jerk.

We once read a critical review of a beachfront hotel in the Caribbean based on the fact that the sand on the seabed was "bumpy."

Whatever the reason, once you've been in business for a while, it's inevitable that your business is going to receive some negative reviews. It doesn't matter that they only account for 0.001% of your clientele because most of your satisfied patients will never get around to leaving you a positive review. The ratio of good to bad reviews online may never be representative of your actual patient base.

If you want to see this in action, go to Trip Advisor and look up one of your favorite hotels. We can almost guarantee you'll find a significant number of negative reviews that seem to be describing a completely different hotel from the one you enjoy.

The reason for this is primarily about the numbers. Hotels, by their very nature, receive a large volume of customers. If one in a thousand has a bad experience and leaves a negative review, but only 10 of the satisfied 999 leave a good review, then that means around 10% of all the comments posted will be negative.

To make it worse, the good reviews are often brief, along the lines of "Had a great stay, highly recommended," whereas the negative reviews often consist of 1,000 words of vitriol describing in excruciating detail every aspect of their dissatisfaction.

And numbers are only part of the problem. It's not unheard of for hotels to try to skewer the competition by posting fake reviews. Or for disgruntled former employees to try to sabotage their previous employer.

Welcome to the Internet. Welcome to our world.

As leaders in online reputation management and SEO, our websites are #1 on Google's organic search results for several competitive reputation management keywords. In fact, we wrote a book about this topic entitled Reputation Management 911: Defuse Online Attackers & Disarm Dishonest Competitors.

Enhancing and defending your reputation on the "Interwebs" is a very real problem that you need to address. We've advised doctors, surgeons, hospitals, lawyers, law firms, dentists, restaurants, franchises and Fortune 500 companies who have suffered significant losses based on what appears to be negative reviews and a bad online reputation.

A common solution is to find incentives for customers to post good reviews but the best you can hope for with this approach is to dilute the problem.

Strange as it may seem, the most effective way to tackle this problem is to publish a book. This works for two reasons. Firstly, the trust and credibility will go a long way to countering the impact of some poor reviews. The fact is, almost every doctor who has been in business for a while will eventually garner some negative reviews. And when all doctors are more or less in the same position, the individual searching for a surgeon is left looking for another factor on which to make a decision.

If you and the three other surgeons in your area all have 90% good reviews, but you're the only one who's published a book, that's an excellent differentiator.

Secondly, the review sites rank well in Google because they're viewed as authority websites. But on this scale they fall a long way behind Amazon. Since Amazon.com has a Google PageRank of 9 out of 10, Amazon is highly trusted and authoritative in the eyes of the search engine. The effect, presuming you've optimized your Amazon book page and Amazon author page correctly, is that when someone searches for your name or targeted keyword (also the name of your book!), the search results, instead of showing your website followed by a bunch of review sites, will often show your practice website followed by the websites that are selling your book such as Amazon and Barnes and Noble.

Where are the review sites? They've been pushed down onto page two of the search results, the place where the vast majority of searchers never bother to look.

Job done.

Would you sign on to a marketing strategy if you knew it would gain you one additional patient per year?

The answer probably depends on how well you're doing at this moment in time but for the purposes of this consideration it's actually irrelevant. Assuming the strategy is within your budget, any marketing push that adds at least one additional patient per year is well worth taking.

Because that one extra patient could be a $30,000 case and a lifelong customer. That one extra client, over the next few years could bring in two or three friends and family members, who could each become lifelong customers and bring in additional referrals of their own. That one extra patient pushes you a little bit further ahead of your competition. That one extra patient keeps your business growing instead of remaining static.

You'd be amazed at the number of marketing strategies that produce absolutely no results. So that one extra client per year? That's a result.

Here's the thing.

Publishing a book ISN'T a marketing strategy... Publishing a book is a tool that gives you access to

DOZENS of different marketing strategies... And every single one of them, on their own, is capable of giving you at least one additional patient per year.

Minimum.

Some of these strategies, starting with the one discussed in the next chapter, are capable of producing tens, hundreds, even thousands of new patients.

Are you starting to grasp the possibilities here? One book...endless benefits.

"We need BIG bold marketing ideas to get more new patients...not small minded tactics that worked 5 years ago."

Scan this QR Code to share with colleagues.

TWO'S COMPANY - THREE'S GOOD BUSINESS SENSE

T HIS CHAPTER IS KEY.

Put aside every distraction, right now, and give the next few pages your close, undivided attention.

Publishing your book and utilizing this strategy effectively could mean the difference between a slight bump in your profits and an overwhelming patient surge that necessitates the need to hire more staff and invest in an additional office.

Here's what you're going to do…

Once you've absorbed everything in this book and you have the plan clearly in mind, you're going to find two referring sources (family medicine docs, internal medicine docs, dermatologists, concierge medicine docs, ob-gyns, infertility docs, cancer surgeons, divorce attorneys, estate planning attorneys or private wealth managers) and collaborate in the production of your book.

So, for example, if you're a plastic surgeon, you could "partner up" and co-author a book with a successful concierge medicine doctor and a successful divorce attorney in your local market.

Each of you is going to produce a book, based on your own specialty and then the three of you are going to combine your work into one compendium that each of you can use to promote your individual practices.

Yes, I appreciate you may not like the idea of sharing the acclaim of producing a book, but there are VERY good reasons why you want to do this.

Please don't dismiss this as an unnecessary complication. The power of book collaboration with two other professionals is huge. And it's this method that is going to open up the door to a massive reservoir of untapped potential.

Consider just four advantages...

#1 – Wider Marketing Reach

When you are featured in a book with two other referring doctors or professionals that do not compete with your practice, you instantly triple your potential marketing reach.

Instead of your book, featuring your name, photograph, and expertise, sitting in just one waiting room, your book now sits in three offices in your local market. Instead of being featured on one practice website, it now is featured on three. Instead of sitting on the bookshelves of one group of prospective patients, your book now resides in the homes of three groups of prospective patients.

And that's just for starters. Consider what happens when your colleagues use the book for other marketing ventures.

If one of your colleagues sends the book to local journalists in the hope of generating some publicity, your name and expertise goes along as well. If one of your colleagues uses the book to gain speaking engagements, your profile sits right alongside his (or hers) and, by association, gains residual credibility.

In fact, every time one of your colleagues does ANYTHING marketing-related with the book, you reap at least some of the rewards.

The work required to produce a book collectively is virtually the same as producing a book solo, but it can easily triple your marketing reach. This is especially true if one of your colleagues is a little better than you at leveraging the book. Every time one of the three of you scores a win, everyone benefits.

It's entirely possible for the three of you, by combining your efforts, to completely dominate your geographical area and secure your long-term success.

#2 – More Referrals For Everyone

It doesn't matter if you're a plastic surgeon, all three of you will benefit from each other's marketing reach. But it can't be denied that there is an added advantage to the specialist.

If, for example, you're a plastic surgeon and one of your two colleagues is an internist, it stands to reason that you dramatically increase the likelihood that referrals are going to flow your way.

Obviously you can't financially incentivize referrals, and the internist will usually want to limit his liability by recommending more than one surgeon, but it's inevitable that the strongest recommendation will be towards their co-author.

It would actually be weird if they didn't.

Even if the internist doesn't tell his patients outright that you're his preferred plastic surgeon, the fact that you're in the book with this person is an implicit endorsement. It's saying "I know and trust this person well enough to co-author a book with him or her so of course I trust this doctor with my patients."

The likelihood is that all three of you will pass referrals to each other but it's no secret that the internist has most of the referring power in these situations. This is why forming a close professional relationship with the doctors that send you referrals is so important if you want to ensure that this transfer of business continues.

And really, what could be better for cementing your relationship than by co-authoring and "partnering" on the publication of a book.

Whether you're looking to strengthen the connection between your primary referral sources or to establish a new connection with a local doctor or professional, collaborating together on a book is one of the most effective methods of increasing the number of referrals you receive.

#3 – Social Proof Among Experts

Even though the three of you will be producing your

own segment individually, by publishing them together you effectively form a three-way endorsement.

In other words, everything you write in your book will carry more weight with the reader because you have two other professionals who clearly trust you and your work. This endorsement is implied by the nature of the book, but you can also state it explicitly by each writing a foreword for each other's segments explaining why you're working with this particular individual and why you respect them and their work.

Reading something like that in black and white is incredibly powerful and results in the trust and credibility imparted by the project becoming greater than the sum of its parts.

#4 – Shared Effort (And Costs)

For reasons that we will discuss in the next chapter, digital publishing on platforms such as the Amazon Kindle, Barnes and Noble Nook and Apple iBookstore is simply not enough. You must also produce physical copies of your book.

The issue is, when a book is published, whether it's in hardback or paperback, anything less than 10,000 words is going to feel rather flimsy. Producing a work, even of this minimum length is a serious undertaking.

However, if the three of you each commit to producing something around the 10,000-15,000 word mark, this is much more manageable, and your combined book will have a substantial feel to it. And don't worry. If you're thinking that even writing 10,000-15,000 words is beyond you, we'll show you a simple way in a few moments.

Costs are also shared through this system. Producing a combined book will cost more than a single work on its own but, once you split the costs three ways, the investment required by each person is significantly less. Although if you're seeking a commitment from a doctor that you're really keen to establish a relationship with, you could offer to split their side of the costs or subsidize their portion entirely.

Remember we said publishing a book is a short-term and long-term strategy rolled into one? This is a great example of that.

In the short-term, you're forging a great relationship with two other non-competing professionals. And when they realize the benefits of this strategy, how grateful do you think they will be to you for approaching them with the idea?

And in the long-term...well, that book is going to stick around for a very long time at every Point-Of-Influence: on waiting-room tables, on the reception desk, on the patient coordinator's desk, on patient bookshelves and in online bookstores.

Most importantly, the book resides on the doctor's home and work office desks establishing top of mind awareness of you and your practice. Even after the initial marketing push is completed, the book will keep working its magic, bringing you new leads and working to build your trusted authority status. To stay fresh and modern, every so often you can update the content with new procedures featuring cutting edge equipment and the latest research findings supporting your specialty. Publishing your second or third edition further builds your authentic authority and expert brand.

Short-term and long-term all rolled into one. Once you get your book project off the ground, this tool is yours to use for years and years to come.

www.PlasticSurgeonMarketingMotto.com

"I really don't have time to figure out the maze of book writing, book publishing, Amazon best seller campaigns, book marketing, SEO and PR."

Scan this QR Code to share with colleagues.

DON'T SCRIMP - CHOOSE HARDCOVER

T HIS IS A REALLY COMMON mistake.
A professional, whatever the industry, decides to self-publish a book and, having looked at the costs, decides to make it a digital-only publication.

Publishing digitally for the Amazon Kindle platform is perfectly fine but if you don't also create a physical book that you can hold in your hand and give away as gifts to your prospects and patients, you're missing out on a whole raft of benefits.

Earlier we mentioned how quickly the digital book market was growing but you may have noticed that the ratio of book sales between physical and digital is only marginally in favor of the latter. So, if you opt for digital publishing only, you're excluding almost half your potential audience.

In the past you'd have to weigh up the costs and benefits, but these days, with the easy availability of "print on demand," this simply isn't an issue. There's no need to purchase a minimum number of copies in advance or maintain stock. You simply publish the book to precise industry formatting standards and deploy the book into the correct global book distribution system. Therefore, whenever someone purchases your book on Amazon or requests your title in a Barnes & Noble store or in another bookstore such as Books A Million, the publisher's print on demand provider prints a copy and ships it directly to Amazon, the Barnes & Noble location or the other bookstore.

This also adds to your credibility. Because you're not limiting yourself to digital outlets, you can make your book available to order and purchase from more than 30,000 different book retailers. You're no longer just an ebook author; you are a real author with a physical book to show for it.

In truth, you shouldn't expect to sell the physical version of the book in massive numbers. Let's face it... you will NOT get rich selling a book on breast augmentation or rhinoplasty. You WILL get rich giving your hard cover book away to prospective patients and referral partners.

This is about maintaining your own personal stock of hardcover books to utilize as your marketing bibles.

To begin with, you'll want to place a few copies on all your coffee tables in your reception area and waiting-rooms.

A copy for each of your staff members to take home and read, in addition to being a nice gesture, is important to ensure everyone related to your business (aka practice) is clear on what you're aiming to achieve.

A small supply of books to send to local, regional and national journalists and industry professionals you want to connect with is an excellent use of this resource. Don't forget to have your staff follow-up and explain your availability and what you have to offer in the way of media interviews and public speaking.

And, most important of all, you need to keep a healthy book supply to give away as gifts to your prospects and patients, especially those who are new or who are still considering treatment.

This is an extremely effective way to keep your patients loyal, increase the likelihood that they'll accept treatment and leave them more inclined to recommend you to others.

Why would giving a patient a book accomplish all of that?

It has to do with a psychological and cultural phenomenon called "reciprocation." Google it if you want to learn more about it but the short version is that when someone gives us a gift of any kind, we feel that, on some level, we owe that person something in return.

It's the reason why charities soliciting by direct mail give you a free pen or a set of address labels; they know that when they do this the volume and value of donations goes up. It's the reason why restaurants give you free mints after your meal; it increases the size of the tip. And it's the reason why Hare Krishna representatives give away free flowers; people are more inclined to give a donation, even if they had zero interest in doing so before, and even if they don't want the flower and immediately discard it.

You might struggle to believe that this really works, especially when almost everyone believes they're unaffected by this ploy. In just the same way, no one really believes they're influenced by advertising. True, this strategy doesn't work on everyone, but it does work on most people and the effect is measurable.

For example, Cialdini's book Influence: The Psychology Of Persuasion discusses how controlled tests were carried out on restaurant diners. The study showed that when a server gave a diner a mint at the end of a meal, average tips went up by 3%.

But when the server gave the diner two mints… Average tips went up by an incredible 14%!

Even more remarkable, if the server gave the diner a mint, made as if to walk away, and then turned back and said, "you know what, here's a second mint for being such a great customer…"

Tips went up by 23%. Because of a mint?

No, because of the power of reciprocation. The value or nutritional content of the mint was irrelevant next to the desire of the diners to return one favor for another, no matter how disproportionate.

So, when you give your book away as a complimentary gift to your patients you're tapping into that reciprocation effect and, at some point in the future, you're going to reap the rewards. It could mean the difference between someone accepting or refusing a recommended treatment. It could encourage a customer to remain a patient despite learning of a new doctor who charges 5% less. And when someone asks that person to recommend a doctor, it could encourage them to talk you up and send you a referral, already warmed up and eager to get started.

And you know what we're going to say next, right?

Even if the patient never reads it, the simple fact of being given the book as a gift is enough to activate the reciprocation effect.

Of course you want them to read the book. It will help to increase their opinion of your expertise and provide them with valuable information on the treatments you provide. But it's important to understand that it isn't a requirement for you to benefit and so it isn't necessary to try to judge whether the person is really interested or likely to read it.

Just hand over the free gift and let the book do the work.

That said, there are a few things you need to keep in mind if this is going to work to maximum effect.

- Don't leave a stack of books on display and invite customers to take a copy. Instead hand them a copy personally. In fact, write a personal note in the front of the book and sign it for them. If the patient feels that they're getting special treatment, it increases the value of the free gift in their eyes (just like the waiter giving an extra mint as a "special favor"). This process should appear spontaneous, organic and authentic to the recipient of the "gifted" book. This offering should not seem robotic, generic or feel like a systemized "sales" process.

- The book's $26 retail price is printed next to the bar code on the back of the book which helps to increase the perceived value of the gift. In fact, Amazon and Barnes & Noble's website will display the publisher's $26 list price validating the perceived value of the book.

- If there's a particular portion of the book you want them to read, make sure you draw their attention to it and perhaps leave a custom bookmark in there so they can easily find it. Even better, look around the immediate area for some scrap paper that can be used as a bookmark. But, instead personally fold and "dog ear" the special chapter to achieve what appears to be a spontaneous helpful gesture.

- Most importantly of all, makes sure the copies that you're giving away are in hardback format.

This final point is critical. Every copy of the book that you give away should be a hardback version and not a paperback version…unless you are utilizing your book in a direct mail campaign. Why? One word: gravitas. A flimsy paperback book is only a small step up from a booklet or brochure and may be quickly dismissed and forgotten.

A hardback book has a greater perceived value in every scenario you can think of. It's the difference between buying someone a box of Oreos and baking them a chocolate cake. It just looks as if more thought and effort has gone into the production.

If your book is in paperback, your patient may decide not to bother reading it and then throw it in the trash. Or they'll read the book… and still throw it in the trash.

But a hardback book? Not only is it more likely that the patient will actually take the time, at the very least, to have a flick through the pages, but it's also very unlikely that they'll throw it away. Far more likely, they'll put it on a bookcase where it's accessible again in the future and easily available if they want to lend it to a friend.

The impact of the hardback format is also felt when sending the book to journalists and other influencers in your marketplace. To try to stand out and get attention, many doctors engaging in PR send an email, a PDF file, a press kit, or even worse, a generic press release blasted out by an online press release distribution service. (To understand how certain online press release distribution services can destroy getting real publicity and can ruin your authority status in the market, please read our other book entitled Reputation Management 911: Defuse Online Attackers & Disarm Dishonest Competitors.) When you send a copy of your hardback book to the journalist or editor to read, review and keep, you stand out as someone willing to go that extra mile, not to mention incredibly generous.

Technology has improved to the point where there's no financial or logistical reason why you can't have it all. Publish a digital version for Amazon Kindle, Apple iPad, and Barnes & Noble Nook AS WELL AS a printed hardcover version and you can hit every demographic at the same time.

www.PlasticSurgeonMarketingMotto.com

"Typically, I don't accept magic beans as payment for rhinoplasty and calf implant surgery."

Scan this QR Code to share with colleagues.

MORE WAYS TO LEVERAGE YOUR BOOK

W E'VE COVERED THE CORE BENEFITS of
publishing a book but we're still only scratch-
ing the surface. The problem is that if we were to fully
explore EVERY avenue this strategy opens up to you,
this book would be a War and Peace-scale epic.

So think of this chapter as the cliff notes of business
benefits beyond just your book. Below is a brief description of the different ways you can leverage and mon-
etize your book, including reminders of those we've
already touched upon (such as the main strategies for
Publicity-Getting, Referral-Getting, Speaking Engage-
ment-Getting, Case Acceptance-Boosting and Celeb-
rity-Building). If you want to explore any of them in
more detail, you'll find our contact information within

this book or just watch our educational webinar presentation at www.GetMorePlasticSurgeryPatients.com.

By the way, this isn't an exhaustive list, but there's more than enough here to create a massive, positive impact on your practice and your bottom line.

Justify Premium Pricing

You need to charge premium prices because you're a highly-qualified expert and authority and you have no desire to mix it up with the hacks or sharks and become locked into a price war that benefits no one.

But you need to be able to justify your prices.

You know that your patients are better with you than someone who is trying to perform complex surgical procedures with minimal training and experience. But communicating that is a challenge.

This is where your book comes in. You don't even have to specifically talk about price within the pages. Just discuss, in explicit detail, the level and depth of training you've undertaken, the quality and benefits of the materials and technology you utilize, and the advanced methods you use to minimize and control pain, and you'll experience far less resistance to your price points.

The power of being a published author will also

play well in this regard. Because you'll be seen as an authority and someone who is at the forefront of their profession, people will expect your prices to be higher than average.

And if they're expecting it, then when it comes to the discussion of costs they'll be mentally prepared and ready to justify it to themselves because they REALLY want to engage you and your team to achieve optimal health and wellness.

Waiting Room Priming

Leave a few copies of your book in your waiting room for patients to browse. This is the ultimate in soft-selling because it allows you to talk about the procedures and treatments you offer without being overtly promotional.

Having the book clearly on display will also allow every patient to become aware of your publication and draw their own conclusions on what this says about your authority and expertise.

Cementing Customer Loyalty

Gifting a copy of your book will help convert prospects into new patients as well as transform existing patients into loyal customers who become die-hard, faithful, "patient for life" raving fans.

When you give the book to the patient, explain why you wrote it (to help patients make the right choices, to answer their most common questions, and to warn them about some of the less effective treatment alternatives), and highlight the portion of the book in which you think they'll be most interested.

And to really seal the deal and ensure the book will never be discarded, write a friendly, personalized message in the front of the book.

**Dear Jen, I wish you all the health
and wellness in the world!
I hope this book answers any other
questions you may have.
Sincerely, Dr. Sara**

Protect Your Patients

When you tell a patient about some of the dangers of using other types of procedures, they might believe you or they might think you're spinning a yarn to convince them to use your practice.

Yet, somehow, when you say the same thing in a

book, it has a completely different feel. Seeing the truth in black and white always has a greater impact and sticks in their minds much longer.

You can also use the book to go into much more detail about some of the dangers of using cheap materials or falling for "bait and switch" selling tactics. Relating specific stories and case studies will also add to the credibility of what you're saying about your treatment philosophy.

Encourage Action

People don't know what they don't know.

For example, the person in need of breast reduction may have no idea that unless they take action quickly their ability to exercise, walk and enjoy life could be damaged. Sure you've explained it to them but they were in a heightened state of stress and anxiety during the consultation to take it in.

But when they read it in your book while sitting at home or in your waiting room, the message written in black and white is much clearer.

And with your book circulating online and offline, you never know when someone will pick it up, learn something new and be encouraged to take action and consider one of your recommended treatments.

Breakdown Barriers

There are certain questions that patients are reluctant to ask either because they're embarrassed, they worry about looking ignorant or because they fear your response will be to recommend some agonizing treatment that they'll feel compelled to agree to.

Questions about pain, healing, scarring and recovery that they vaguely remember hearing about, may be straightforward to you but awkward and uncomfortable for the patient.

A book allows you to address these issues in depth, as well as any other concerns that you wish to focus on, so that the patient can review the material in private.

Empowered by their new found knowledge, your patients will be more relaxed and much more open to considering treatment options.

Star Power

Your picture on the front or back cover of your hardback book, your words quoted in a local newspaper article, your live interview on a morning health segment on a real television news show (not a fake info-mercial)... all of these will provide you celebrity status.

This adjustment in the way you are viewed by your patients will happen naturally and will do amazing things to the trust and credibility that people assign to you.

However, to take full advantage of this, don't be afraid to showcase your success. Make sure copies of your book are always on display in your reception area, waiting rooms, patient coordinator offices and exam rooms. And when you're featured in the news media, highlight this information on your website, your brochures, framed reprints for the reception area walls and in future editions of your book. "As Seen On...", "As Featured In...", and "As Interviewed On..." are all powerful statements that imply trusted third party endorsements, regardless of the brevity of your Publicity/PR success.

Preferred Provider

As we all know, compensating doctors for sending you referrals is illegal, which is why you need a strategy that goes beyond merely asking.

Co-authoring a book with other doctors or specialists forges long-lasting ties between you, virtually guarantees you ongoing referrals and makes it highly likely that you will become the primary recommended plastic surgeon.

More Patient-To-Patient Referrals

Referrals from patients can be hard to come by and, although your book will increase your opportunities in this area, you don't have to sit around and hope.

Just ask your patients if they'll recommend you... utilizing your book for reciprocation.

If you've just completed a highly successful procedure, few people are going to object to this request. Whether or not they'll actually remember or be inclined to do it is another matter. Remember, some people won't be keen to advertise the fact that they've just had a major surgical procedure.

This is where your book seals the deal. Give them a second copy (presuming you've already given them their own copy earlier, before you performed surgery) and ask them to pass it on to anyone they know who's just like them and shares their past health experience and might benefit.

Reciprocation comes into play again. You've now

given them, not one, but two copies of your book. They're not going to be at peace until they've figured out whom to give this second copy of your book to and delivered it as promised.

Do this with every patient who experiences your surgical mastery and is pleased with the results. Shortly, you'll have copies of your book circulating in homes throughout the metro area. Your book becomes an automated mechanism for offline Word-Of-Mouth marketing.

Online Lead Generator

Most of the business world has caught up to the fact that their website needs a method for capturing leads, a system that enables visitors to enter their email addresses and receive periodic marketing communications.

What most haven't yet figured out is that very few people hand over their contact info without a really good incentive or offer (also commonly referred to as Opt-In Bait or a Lead Magnet). Here's a hint: "Subscribe To Our Newsletter" isn't going to get the job done.

Can you use your book as an incentive to encourage

your website visitors to give you their email address or mobile phone number?

Absolutely!

Here's how you do it…

Feature the hardback version of your book on your website as being available on Amazon for $26. Include a link so people can click through and see that it is actually for sale. This is known as third party validation. If Amazon is selling your $26 list price book for $18, then it must be worth between $18 and $26 because Amazon says so. Next to that link on your website, invite your visitors to obtain a FREE audio mp3 download version of the book. All they have to do is enter their name and email address and an audio version of your book will be sent to their inbox.

No matter what kind of email subscriber rate you're getting right now, we can virtually guarantee that this Lead Magnet offer will dramatically increase your email opt-in conversion rate.

Another great reason to make this "opt-in bait" available is in preparation for your TV and radio appearances. Most hosts will be quite relaxed about allowing you to mention your book (you are, after all, appearing on their program without charge) which is also your opportunity to invite the viewers or listeners to visit your website for a free download of the book, inside of which they'll learn the truth about liposuction, face lifts or arm lifts.

Now your media coup is not only providing you with valuable PR, it's also directly bringing in email leads that you can cultivate and convert into patients.

Hassle-Free Testimonials And Reviews

In a perfect world, every satisfied patient would pause before leaving your office and say, "Hey, would you like me to write you a testimonial?"

Never going to happen, right? So, unless you want to wait ten years before you have enough customer comments to make it worth adding to your website, you and your staff are going to have to start asking.

Yes, we know it's awkward, but it's also important. You need a page on your website called "<Your Practice Name / Doctor's Name> – Reviews" so that when people perform a Google search on that keyword phrase they're more likely to find your website page than that venue for unhinged miscreants that is the free-for-all review site.

The good news is that your book makes it easy

to obtain testimonials and removes almost all of the awkwardness.

Step 1: Every time you give a free copy of your book to a prospect or a patient, make a note of it.

Step 2: The next time that patient is in your office, at the end of the visit say, "Hey, remember that book I gave you last time? I'm putting together a second edition and I was wondering if you would mind providing me with a testimonial to go in or on the back cover of my book."

Step 3: After the patient readily agrees (reciprocation, remember?), give them a short testimonial form to fill in. Success!

But, whatever you do, don't ask the person if they read your book. Most won't have done more than flick through a few pages and you'll be forcing them to either lie or go through the awkwardness of admitting they haven't got round to it yet. If they read it and enjoyed it, they'll tell you unprompted, so just leave the question out of the conversation.

And if they haven't read the book and agree to leave you a testimonial anyway, that's up to them. You can remove the ethical dilemma by wording the form so that they can choose to leave a comment about your book OR your practice.

PR Positioning

Send your hardcover book to targeted healthcare journalists at local, regional, and national media outlets. A proportion of the recipients, particularly on a local level, will be impressed by the gesture and will remember you as THE AUTHORITY AND THE EXPERT when they're next running a story related to plastic surgery or aesthetics.

They may contact you and ask if they can run a quote from your book. Naturally, you'll agree, but make sure you take the opportunity to let them know that you're available to provide opinions, phone interviews, sound bites, quotes, live studio interviews or anything else that they need.

Of course, you can do all of that without writing a book but, if a journalist has the choice of doctors to call upon, he or she's far more likely to contact the one who's written a book on the subject. It just naturally positions you as the authority on the topic.

When you score major media coverage (a feature article on your practice or quote in a health story in a prominent media outlet), don't just sit back and gloat. Write a press release about your achievement but angle it so that it focuses, not on you, but on the topic covered by the journalist who featured you and include your comments on the coverage. Distribute the press release via PRNewswire or BusinessWire (NOT PRWeb) to leverage the initial publicity into more news coverage. We call this re-merchandizing the news.

Next, write a quick "thank you" note to the journalist who interviewed you. Here are some guidelines. Include your business card so they add you to their "sources" rolodex. Do NOT thank them for the "free" publicity. They are not in the business of giving you free advertising and promoting your business. A journalist's duty is to inform, educate and communicate with his or her readers. Thank them for their accurate reporting and interesting news angle. Let them know you are always available to speak on the record or on background if they are researching a health related story. This follow- up will make it far more likely that you'll become their "go to guy" or "go to girl" for future stories.

Speaking Engagements

Marketing one-to-one can be a laborious process. However, marketing one-to-many is a much more efficient use of your time. Being interviewed on your local ABC, CBS, FOX or NBC affiliate TV morning shows or national broadcast news shows such as CBS This Morning, CNN, FOX News, Good Morning America, MSNBC or the Today Show is an effective one-to-many marketing strategy. Speaking to a group of prospects such as affluent retirees or business executives potentially in need of cosmetic enhancements can also be an amazing one-to-many marketing opportunity.

Becoming a published author is the first step in getting you on the radar of event organizers, meeting planners and associations. There's no point in waiting to be invited; have your staff start making phone calls on your behalf to decision makers at assisted living communities, homeowners associations, chambers of commerce, rotary clubs, lions clubs, country clubs, local medical and hospital associations, continuing education events, medical study clubs and even companies that sell medical equipment.

This is where your book helps you out beyond simply establishing you as an authority.

It also gives you a REASON to ask for speaking engagements.

If you call up an event organizer and say you'd like to speak to their group because you want to promote your practice, you're not going to get very far. But if, instead, you tell them about your newly published book and you'd like to speak to their group about the health benefits of the latest advancements in breast reduction…

That's a completely different story.

In both cases you're speaking with a promotional motive, but when that motivation is based around a book it creates a completely different impression.

Instead of telling his group that local board certified periodontist, Dr. Jason Stoner, is going to talk to them about his practice, the event organizer is going to tell his group that local author, Dr. Jason Stoner, is going to talk to them about his book LANAP Laser Gum Surgery. This is all about Frame and Positioning.

Can you see how different this proposition is?

You're essentially camouflaging your pitch through your book and, even though some people will know this is the case, you'll be amazed how few people will really care. They've bagged a published author to speak at their event and that trumps pretty much everything else.

Whether or not you sell or give away your book at an event or speaking engagement is between you and the organizer and will also depend on the nature of your audience. Any way you can get your hard cover book in the hands of your target market (prospective patients in need of your surgical solutions) will be a huge win for your practice.

www.PlasticSurgeonMarketingMotto.com

"I am the CEO of Lifestyle Lift® and I want you to work for me now..."

Scan this QR Code to share with colleagues.

THE PLAN:

FROM STRATEGY TO PUBLICATION

www.PlasticSurgeonMarketingMotto.com

"Does this patient need a rhinoplasty revision or is that chocolate on the x-ray?"

Scan this QR Code to share with colleagues.

BRING THE PAIN

I F YOU WERE TO COMPILE all the advertising and marketing material from plastic surgeons all over the country you would be forgiven for thinking that all that matters is having the perfect nose and flawless skin.

If you were to interview plastic surgeons, up and down the country, and get them to talk about what they believe to be important, you'd be forgiven for thinking that all that matters is education, experience, and technologically advanced equipment.

If you were to interview patients, across all demographics, about their aesthetic concerns, you'd be forgiven for thinking that all that matters is how much a procedure costs.

And yet all of those matters take a distant second

place to the one fundamental issue that very few seem to want to talk about. Pain...or the fear of pain during the recovery process.

It's the proverbial elephant in the room. Surgeons sometimes forget about it because their priority is the health of the patient; marketers avoid it because they don't want to remind people that medical procedures and the healing process can be uncomfortable; patients don't want to talk about it for fear of sounding like a wimp.

And yet, although costs, proficiency, health, and aesthetics are very important, all of those things become virtually redundant if you address this one simple psychological element.

This is what it's all about. How much and for how long is it going to throb afterwards? How big is the scar going to be? How much pain medication will I need to take? Why do you have to break my nose? How many nerves are you going to jangle? How much blood is there going to be? How long am I going to be sipping soup through a straw? What if the surgery doesn't work and does not meet my expectations? What if surgery doesn't go as planned?

To a greater or lesser degree these are the, often unspoken, thoughts of every one of your patients, and represent the greatest barrier to accepting your recommended treatment and scheduling surgery.

To illustrate how significant this issue is, consider this:

A patient has a choice between two virtually identical procedures. Which do you think they'll choose?

Procedure Cost: $10,000
Surgeon A: 20 Years Private Practice
Results: Nearly Perfect
Pain: Excruciating Agony During Recovery

Procedure Cost: $20,000
Surgeon B: 10 Years Private Practice
Results: Almost Perfect
Pain: Virtually Painless Recovery

With the fluke exception of a person who is ridiculously tight with their money, everyone is going to choose Surgeon B.

It's not that surgeon experience, results and cost aren't important; it's simply that, even when combined, they all take a backseat to the issue of pain.

What conclusion should we draw from this?

That your book should discuss surgeon experience, results, and cost, but that it should also dedicate a sizeable portion to discussing the subject of pain. Perhaps even making it a central theme.

Be the one surgeon in your area who isn't afraid to discuss the subject. Acknowledge the patient's concerns, be honest about the typical pain and discomfort experienced during recovery with a specific procedure, and then go into great depth about all the different ways you are able to limit and remove the pain.

If you can allay patients' fears in this regard, your ability to turn prospects into patients is going to soar.

Your honesty will also pay dividends.

If one doctor says he can perform a procedure that yields little to no pain during recovery, but you, by contrast, explain that there will be discomfort due to ABC but that you minimize it by performing XYZ, you will come off as more believable and, therefore, infinitely more trustworthy.

Conceding that some discomfort is possible also sets up patients' expectations in the right order. Far better that they expect some pain and experience none or very little, than expect a totally pain-free experience and suffer even a small amount of pain.

You should also reinforce your discussion of the pain issue by showing video testimonials from previous patients commenting on their experience. For the same reasons as discussed above, don't only include comments from patients who experienced no pain; throw in a few from those who felt a little discomfort but were very satisfied overall.

Another angle from which to discuss pain is to highlight the reader's opportunities to avoid it altogether by making the right decisions now. An obvious example would be that agreeing to Procedure X now will reduce the likelihood of having to undergo the more painful Procedure Y or Z in the future. These scenarios have to be explained to the prospective patient in precise detail using what we call influence and persuasion language and vocabulary (aka words that sell). In addition to the specific language and vocabulary, plastic surgeons and their patient coordinators must utilize a distinct voice tonality and pattern in the delivery of those words. Remember this: It is not just what you say...it is not just what people hear...**it is how you make people feel**. We have developed a training course for doctors and their staff members on utilizing psychological buying triggers called **Stealth Selling Strategies To Convert More Prospects Into Patients**. To learn more about our training system, please view the presentation located at **www.PatientGettingStrategies.com**.

You could also talk about the pain that can come with being treated by an inadequately experienced or qualified doctor. Some subtlety is required here; you don't want to come across as overly critical. Describing procedures you've performed to fix the mistakes performed by other surgeons is a smart way to imply that pain can be avoided by choosing you as the practitioner in the first place.

And bear in mind that pain comes in lots of different guises. Overpaying is painful, losing work days through long recovery times is painful, having to avoid certain foods is painful and social awkwardness due to an imperfect nose or excess wrinkles, can be the most agonizing pain of all.

Use these themes to demonstrate your understanding of people's fears and then prove your ability to remove them.

Be selective with your discussion of pain. Overuse can come across as scaremongering or negative. But judicious application of this argument will make your book powerful and highly effective in motivating the reader to take the desired action.

www.PlasticSurgeonMarketingMotto.com

"How did Dr. Smith get his breast implants book on the first page of Google?"

Scan this QR Code to share with colleagues.

MAKE IT PERSONAL

ONE OF THE DRAWBACKS OF being perceived as an expert and an authority is that you create a distance between yourself and your prospects and patients.

People will respect your abilities and your achievements but they'll also feel a little removed from you as a person.

And while their trust in you as a doctor will go up, their trust in you as a person can go down.

It sounds a little weird but it's a natural human reaction. We trust people we know and relate to because, to a certain degree, we can predict their behavior. But when someone is outside of our sphere of understanding, even to a small degree, this has an impact.

People will trust that you know what you're talking

about in cosmetic health matters or aesthetics but they may also feel some doubt as to whether they can trust your advice. Think about this scenario: You're smart enough to manipulate them to accept treatment that they may not really want or need. We all know you would never dream of taking advantage of your patients, but a seed of doubt may still lie in the minds of the people you treat.

Exactly the same thing happens when people speak to lawyers, celebrities, and politicians. We respect their skills but we also feel a bit wary of them as a person.

Whether you're aware of it or not, the fact that you're a doctor and wear a white coat or scrubs is already enough to have created this effect. But when you publish a book and become a local celebrity, this result can be enhanced.

This phenomenon is relatively minor and the drawbacks are easily outweighed by the benefits, but that doesn't mean you should shrug your shoulders and do nothing.

Especially when there is an easy fix.

All you have to do is devote a portion of your book to share your personal story. You must craft and communicate your aspirational narrative because people engage with a good compelling personal story. This is a combination of story telling and story selling.

Hang on guys. Weren't you just saying that the book shouldn't be overtly self-promotional?

Yes, but there is a world of difference between promoting your qualifications as a surgeon and promoting your qualifications as a human being.

We're talking about dropping in anecdotes about how your grandfather inspired you, the moment you met your wife or husband in college, and maybe that time you reversed your first car into a lamppost. Because when you do this, aside from adding color to your book, it reminds the reader that you're a normal human being who has hopes, dreams, family, friends, hobbies, and even embarrassing stories (obviously avoid talking about blunders connected to your profession).

This humanizes you and, more importantly, allows people to connect with you. Without human connection, you will not sell. What we stated earlier is worth repeating: It is not just what you say, it is how you make people feel. Even if it's subconscious, readers will recognize that in certain areas you are just like their brother, sister, son, daughter, mother or father, or even just like them.

Even if you play golf and your reader plays tennis, these nuggets of information bring you back into people's comfort zone without impacting on their perception of your expertise.

Now you're no longer just an expert surgeon. You're also an expert surgeon that people feel comfortable with and, most importantly, are inclined to trust...with their health.

Trust, Authenticity and Believability are critical elements to closing any sale such as when patients are in a position to accept or delay treatment. After conducting in depth off-the-record research interviews with a variety of patients from many different medical practices, we have found that the majority of prospective patients experience a sense of high anxiety, trepidation and nervousness when meeting with a new doctor for the first time. If a prospect is in a state of anxiety and fear during the initial consultation, this causes a roadblock to the sales process and can dramatically decrease patient surgeries. Our marketing solutions firm decided to solve this problem for our clients.

The challenge is: how do we create an emotional bond or connection between prospect and doctor before they ever meet? Our solution is called Patient

Indoctrination Videos. Based on our 20 year history in the film industry and our creative skills for unique cinematic storytelling, Patient Indoctrination Videos influence and persuade prospective patients so that they truly get to Know, Like, Trust and Fall In Love with doctors and their practices BEFORE the initial consultation. Besides just featuring the surgeon in a talking head style format answering the most Frequently Asked Questions (FAQs) and Should Ask Questions (SAQs), these videos humanize the doctor revealing their personal side as they interact with family, patients and staff. We also blend in carefully selected psychological buying triggers as well as compelling testimonials from actual patients and referring doctors. Our cinematic storytelling videos are in many ways like abbreviated feature films that actually detail our doctor clients' personal back stories of struggle and triumph and uncover the foundation for their passion for helping their patients achieve total health and wellness. With offices in both Washington, DC and Los Angeles, our firm has mastered the art and science of manufacturing "great optics" for our clients. We are all about making our clients look and sound amazing.

To watch a $20,000 Patient Indoctrination Video

we produced and filmed for a client AND receive the EXACT step-by-step blueprint on how to script and produce your own, please view the presentation located at **www.PatientIndoctrinationVideo.com**.

"Here is my To-Do List if I want to write a book all by myself, edit it all by myself, publish it all by myself, market it all by myself...and become the recognized authority and expert in my market."

Scan this QR Code to share with colleagues.

DOING IT RIGHT AS A DIYER

THIS SECTION, "THE PLAN," TAKES you through the steps of creating your book, even if you have no ability as a writer and you have limited time. However, if you'd prefer a "Done For You" solution that reduces your time commitment to as little as five hours, you may wish to skip straight to the next section entitled: "The Short Cut."

From the beginning of this book we've hinted at the fact that it's possible to accomplish the writing and publication of your book without having to spend months, or even years, of hard work.

This section will explain, step-by-step, how to accomplish this and take your book from strategy to publication, faster than you ever thought possible.

Now, we're not going to lie, there is still an investment of time required along with a handful of trial and error. But, if you follow these steps carefully, you'll avoid the vast majority of the problems that others struggle with in trying to self-publish and Do It Themselves.

Step One: Gathering Content

The last thing you want to do is just open your laptop and start typing. As they say… "failing to plan is planning to fail." On the other hand, at our firm, we like to say: Plan the work. Work the plan.

Before a single word is written you need to plan exactly what is going to go into your book and gather all of that content together. If you don't do this, you will likely double or triple the time and money you spend on the second phase.

The easiest way to do this is to grab a microphone or camcorder and record yourself talking about the subject of your book. Spend a little time brainstorming, make a list of all the questions and topics you want to cover, and then work your way through each one.

You may find it easier to get one of your partners, associates or assistants to help you with this by acting as an interviewer who can prompt you to expand on certain points or explain a concept in more detail.

Don't worry about talking in perfect sentences or

sound bites. Stumbling over your words, long pauses, and so on, don't matter at all. The only goal here is to get everything out of your head and into audio format.

Step Two: Transcription

Once you have at least five hours (about 25,000 to 30,000 words) of audio content, go online and find a transcriber to turn your speech into text. You'll find these services if you search Google. As a medical professional, you may already have a relationship with a dependable transcription service.

Step Three: Hire A Ghostwriter

No matter how talented a writer you consider yourself to be, please don't make the mistake of thinking you can do this part yourself. Otherwise you'll probably experience one or both of the following:

1. You'll take years to complete the book, or worse, you'll get mired in the process, distracted, and never get around to completing it.

2. Your finished product will be overly technical and unnecessarily dull for your target market: consumers who are prospective patients.

A great ghostwriter will complete your book, based on your transcripts, within about two months, and will add style, verve and humor to the prose.

We don't have to convince you of the importance of hiring a professional. You would never advise a patient to get a medical procedure from a writer who does a little plastic surgery on the side, so don't arrogantly assume that you can do a little writing in your spare time and achieve the same level of quality as someone who has made ghostwriting their career.

Put your ego to one side and hire the best ghostwriter you can afford. High quality ghostwriters charge between $15,000 to $150,000 depending on the length of the book. Once you see the result, completed in a matter of weeks, you'll know you made the right decision.

Take extra time and care when choosing your ghostwriter. Get a few different writers to create a single chapter and then decide which result you like the best and most closely matches your voice.

Once you've chosen your writer, take some time to explain the overall purpose of the book and the topics you want to be the main focus.

Step Four: Push For Completion

Writing for hours on end is mentally tough and even the most experienced writers have a tendency to procrastinate before racing at the last minute to get everything done before the deadline.

To ensure that this doesn't happen to your book, don't instruct your writer and then forget about them. Check in at regular intervals and ask them to send you updates every few chapters so you can review them and provide feedback. DISCLAIMER REMINDER: If this Do It Yourself (DIY) process sounds overly complicated or too time consuming, please skip to the chapter entitled **The Short Cut**.

Step Five: Edit And Proofread

No matter how thrilled you are with the finished work, spend time editing and proofreading. In fact, hire a copy editor and a line editor. This book is being published in your name, so if your ghostwriter has made errors, it will be you that ends up embarrassed.

Don't move on until you're 100% satisfied with the completed text.

Step Six: Design Your Book Cover

Hire a graphic designer with experience in designing book covers so that you can be sure they understand the correct format, and provide them with a few photographs of you in your office setting, as well as a few against a solid background.

Also, hire a professional photographer since it is well worth the investment. The results, as well as being used on your book cover or back cover, can also be featured on your website or in other promotional marketing materials.

Thinking long-term, when you gain some media coverage, it's not unusual to be asked for some high resolution images, so it's always useful to have a selection on standby.

Step Seven: Publish With Amazon

Despite every effort to make the process simple, publishing a Kindle book through Amazon has a bit of a learning curve. So save yourself time and headaches worrying about the right fonts, page sizes, margins, and converting your final manuscript into a .mobi file by hiring a specialist in book layout and design to handle this process.

Step Eight: Publish Everywhere

Leverage a book distribution system that can make your hardcover book and digital book available for purchase in every possible online and offline bookstore. Keep in mind that you want to ensure your book is available to order in actual offline bookstores such as Barnes & Noble and Books A Million. For example, if a prospective patient walks into a book store and can't find your book on the shelves, he or she can ask the sales clerk to order Dr. Jane Smith's plastic surgery book. You need to publish the book to precise industry formatting standards and deploy the book into the correct global book distribution system so that it can be ordered, printed and then delivered to the book store within about two or three business days.

You can research what's available and work your way through dozens of different outlets, or you can hire someone who's already done this hundreds of times to handle the grunt work for you.

By now you know what we recommend.

At this point you'd be forgiven for feeling some concern about the expense of hiring and managing all these different people.

Two things...

First of all, aside from the ghostwriter and book graphic designer, most of the above jobs can be completed for reasonable rates.

Secondly, keep in mind that publishing a book is a long-term sales and marketing strategy. Unless you make a complete mess of the production or fail to utilize the book once it's ready, the investment you make now will pay you back many, many times over.

If in doubt, go back and reread the chapter, "More Ways to Leverage Your Book" to be reminded of all the different ways this is going to benefit you and your practice.

www.PlasticSurgeonMarketingMotto.com

"Let's try the Good Surgeon/Bad Surgeon routine."

Scan this QR Code to share with colleagues.

DOING IT WRONG AS A DIYER

I F YOU TAKE CARE TO hire the right people, you'll avoid most of the common mistakes, but there are a few decisions that fall squarely on your shoulders as a Do It Yourselfer. Below are the three most common mistakes that can kill your book project before it's even hit the virtual shelves.

#1 – Hunting For Cheap Talent

Someone out there, probably somewhere in Eastern Europe, is a literary genius who performs ghostwriting services for just a penny per word.

And your chances of finding this person…? Virtually nil.

Not only is he or she buried within a huge pile of pitifully poor writers, he's also only one or two jobs away from being recognized as a master wordsmith, giving him or her the power to charge a small fortune for their service.

Trying to find genuine talent among the morass of inadequacy is like trying to find a needle in a haystack the size of a small country.

And, ironically, you'll waste so much money in the process that you may as well have just hired a more expensive ghostwriter in the first place.

We know it's a cliché to say that you get what you pay for but it's amazing how many people quickly forget this axiom when they stumble across rock-bottom price freelancers.

It's not a trick. Most of these people may have a long history of satisfied clients. But most of that work consists of junky articles, blog posts and short ebooks where the quality required is merely adequate.

You don't have the luxury of producing something that is passable.

As a professional with impressive qualifications and credentials, every reader that picks up your book will be expecting a standard of prose way beyond your typical copy (text) on a medical website. Your text will be expected to be clever, erudite and grammatically flawless.

A great writer can create this for you. But as you would reasonably expect, the cost is going to be much higher than the average freelancer.

As a general rule of thumb, you get what you pay for. Be prepared to pay anything up to one or two dollars per word for a highly skilled and experienced ghostwriter.

Yes, paying out such a large sum of money is going to sting a little, but you'll soon forget about that when you get a great end result.

You see, the difference between an average ghostwriter and a great ghostwriter is far more than just their ability to write fluent prose.

An average ghostwriter rearranges your transcript into sentences and paragraphs, whereas a great ghostwriter takes the time to research and understand the concepts that you're communicating so they can rewrite it in a manner that is both scholarly and easy for the layperson to understand.

Keep in mind that the finished book is going to have YOUR name on the front. You need to be absolutely, positively thrilled with the results because this is the product that you're going to be giving to patients, colleagues and journalists.

If the book is only mediocre (or worse), the whole project is going to come to a grinding halt. You'll get 100 copies printed up and delivered before finally accepting what you knew all along... That you'd be embarrassed to give your new book to anyone to read.

This is easily the most important mistake to avoid and applies equally to the graphic designer you hire to design your book cover. Ignore the amateurs, hire a professional, and craft a book that you can be proud to put your name to.

#2 – One Long Infomercial

Imagine sending your book to a journalist.

He or she admires the attractive cover design and the reassuring weight of the hardback format.

The journalist opens the book and begins to read...

After reading three chapters that do nothing more than drone on about your credentials, your amazing practice, and your scores of satisfied patients, he closes the book and quickly forgets it ever existed.

Your book is not a brochure for your services or a mechanism for stroking your ego.

Actually, scratch that. To some degree, that's exactly

what it is. But it needs to be so subtle that it's virtually unrecognizable.

You must, absolutely must, focus on content first and everything else second.

If you do a great job of putting together interesting, informative, valuable content, you'll be promoting yourself and your services without having to come right out and say it.

If the book is structured properly there will be opportunities to mention your qualifications, your successes, and even your office, but it needs to be done in such a way that it appears to be a natural part of the story you're telling.

A great ghostwriter will be able to write your book with this format in mind but it's important that when you record your audios you don't devote too much of the time to promotional information. It needs to be in there but not at the expense of compiling informative content.

#3 – Assuming Everything's Good

Once you get the hang of outsourcing it can become a little bit addictive.

When you have a group of good people, all beavering away on your book and producing great results, there's great satisfaction to be had from leaving them to get on with it and trusting in their abilities.

However…

Once again, keep in mind that the finished product will bear your name. And, as a consequence, any mistakes will be attributed to you.

So, before anything goes to print, check every word personally.

Not once. But twice.

Make sure the proofreaders haven't missed anything. Make sure that the factual information is accurate and properly reflects your understanding. And make sure that there is nothing in the content that could come back to bite you.

Maybe you want to tell your readers about surgeons who perform a certain type of plastic surgery without sufficient patient experience. That's fine, but it's not a good idea to mention anyone by name.

Perhaps you have a particular dislike for a certain brand of breast implant… and with good reason. But before you "name and shame," you need to consider whether you're opening yourself to the risk of a libel lawsuit.

Review everything in your book carefully and, if you're in any doubt about a particular passage, either seek legal advice or just leave it out.

Also, don't forget to add a Medical Disclaimer to the front of your book. Here is the one we often utilize but you must seek your own legal advice regarding the creation of your medical disclaimer for your book. We are not attorneys and we do not provide legal advice.

SAMPLE MEDICAL DISCLAIMER

The information presented in this book is for educational and informational purposes only. The content is not intended to be a substitute for professional medical advice, medical diagnosis, or medical treatment. Always seek the advice of your surgeon or other qualified doctor with any questions you may have regarding a medical condition. Please do not disregard professional medical advice or delay in seeking it. The author and publisher of this book disclaim any loss or liability, either directly or indirectly as a consequence of the information presented herein, or the use and application of such information. This book is sold with the understanding that the publisher is not engaged in rendering medical advice.

The one thing that ties all of these three mistakes together is that they're all a reflection of the fact that this book is being published in your name. Being a published author is great for your reputation, providing you don't produce something that could, in some way, denigrate everything you've worked hard to achieve.

Don't be paranoid about these issues, but do take care to give adequate attention to each part of the production process.

www.PlasticSurgeonMarketingMotto.com

"Can our internet marketing firm do that for us?"

Scan this QR Code to share with colleagues.

THE SHORT CUT:

THE 5 HOUR SOLUTION

www.PlasticSurgeonMarketingMotto.com

"I've seen this before. A plastic surgeon marketing consultant paralyzed by poor listening skills."

Scan this QR Code to share with colleagues.

THE PAIN FREE VERSION

I T'S EASY TO SELL PEOPLE on the benefits of becoming a published author.

But excitement soon dies once they realize what is involved in taking the idea from conception to publication.

Maybe this book has had a similar effect on you. Perhaps the first few chapters excited you about the potential of this idea to transform your business, but the previous section was like a bucket of cold water on your enthusiasm.

If so, this section is going to be like a warm, fluffy towel for your expectations.

Hang on. Did we just…?

Did we just spend the last few chapters highlighting the pain of producing a publishable book so that we could spend the next few chapters telling you how we can make this a pain-free experience?

Of course that's what we did!

Look – we're not sharing these marketing techniques with you because we think they sound like a good idea. We're sharing them with you because they work.

When we say that talking to your patients on the subject of pain and how you can minimize their discomfort is a good marketing technique, we're not telling you this because it's cute. We're telling you this because it's effective.

These techniques work for our clients and... guess what...they also work for us.

There's no trickery here.

When you tell a patient that you can minimize their discomfort with specific minimally invasive techniques, you're not conning them. You're offering a genuine solution to a real problem and describing it in a style that gets their attention.

In the same manner, we know that writing and publishing a book is challenging, we know for a fact that we can offer you an easier way, and we're presenting it to you in a fashion that we believe you'll find appealing.

If the advice in this book didn't work we wouldn't be wasting your time with it. Our confidence in it is evidenced by our willingness to use it in our own business. We doubt it's escaped your notice that this very book that you are reading is very much a product of the methodology we've been describing for the last 20,000 words.

We know that this works. And we're so confident that it works that we have absolutely no qualms in being open about the fact that we're using the same approach to convince you of this.

So, here's the bottom line.

Creating and publishing a book <u>on your own</u> is eminently achievable, but you should expect to…

- Put in considerable time and effort hiring people and learning new systems.

- Experience the occasional unreliable freelance service provider.

- Struggle to predict costs accurately.

- Invest considerable time in re-writing and editing your book.

- Learn the ins and outs of the book publishing industry, book marketing and Amazon Kindle and Apple iBooks publishing.

By contrast, hiring us to manage the process on your behalf will allow you to...

Limit your time investment to as little as five hours.

Avoid having to deal with any freelance service providers.

Avoid having to learn any new technology or systems or industries.

Complete the project at a fixed cost with no hidden extras.

We've completed this process for our clients so many times that we now have a system that operates like clockwork. We've assembled and hired a highly-skilled team of writers, proofreaders, and designers. And we have the marketing and management experience to take care of every aspect of this strategy.

Allow us to share with you the exact process we use and why we're perfect to deliver a published product that you'll be proud and delighted to put your name to.

www.PlasticSurgeonMarketingMotto.com

"Since you are the one who suggested we write and publish our own plastic surgery book to build our practice, I suggest you do all the research on how to publish it and market it."

Scan this QR Code to share with colleagues.

FIVE HOURS!

HOW IS IT POSSIBLE THAT you can become a published author in five hours?

Because five hours is all it takes us to interview you and extract the expertise that will go into your book.

After that we handle everything else. And we mean EVERYTHING.

We'll schedule five one-hour phone calls, fitting them in around your schedule and, after that, before you know it, you'll have a completed draft of your book ready for you to review.

Assuming everything is to your satisfaction (and we do an awesome job, so it's highly likely that it will be), a short time later your book will be available for everyone to purchase and your hardcover books will arrive at your office.

Until someone learns how to perform mind- melds there simply isn't a faster way to turn your knowledge into a high quality book that you can use to market your practice.

We'll take care of all the elements described in the previous section, plus a few more. Here's how it works...

Step One: We have an informal chat on the phone so we can understand your practice and your goals. This is a custom service tailored to your needs.

Step Two: We prepare our interview questions and send them to you to review (some like to prepare their responses, others prefer something more extemporaneous – the choice is yours).

Step Three: We conduct the interview in five, one-hour telephone calls.

Step Four: We transcribe the recordings of the phone calls and deliver the results to a senior member of our ghostwriting team (more on this part of the process in the next chapter).

Step Five: After the book has been written, edited, and proofread, we send it to you for your consideration. This is your opportunity to request any adjustments or additions.

Step Six: After the text is edited, finalized and approved by you, we instruct one of our graphic artists to create and design the book cover, the back cover and the spine.

Step Seven: One of our layout designers formats the book interior to our exact publishing and printing requirements keeping in mind we offer the widest range of paper, trim sizes, bindings, hardcover, paperback, and color options. It is then uploaded into the largest book distribution and ordering system so that it is available for sale in nearly 40,000 global booksellers and online retailers.

Step Eight: We order hardcover copies and have them shipped directly to your office (additional copies can be ordered at any time through our print-on-demand service).

The above is the very definition of a "done for you" solution. It's your expertise, your knowledge, even your style (our ghostwriters are excellent at capturing the "voice" of the author), but with minimal disruption to your routine.

And we don't stop there. We also offer additional book marketing services...

Supercharge The Book Launch: We launch your Amazon best seller campaign by coordinating your launch window to maximize the initial burst of sales to achieve #1 Best Seller status - an accolade you can utilize to increase the authority and status of you and your book. In addition, we can provide our clients with best seller campaigns for The New York Times, Wall Street Journal and USA Today.

Page One Of Google: Using our search engine optimization (SEO) services, we'll position your Amazon book webpage (URL) so that it ranks for your targeted keyword on the first page of Google's organic search results. Why do you want your Amazon book URL on Page One of Google for your targeted keyword? Simple...to get more patients! Imagine for a moment that both your website and your Amazon book URL are positioned on Page One of Google. Prospective patients will certainly click the Amazon search result because it is highly trusted by consumers and they wish to discover who in their area actually wrote the book on plastic surgery. Is a prospective patient more likely to schedule an appointment with the surgeon who "wrote the book" on face lifts or breast implants? Absolutely! Although Amazon.com has a Google PageRank of 9 out of 10 (which essentially means the Amazon website is extremely authoritative and trusted in the eyes of Google's algorithm), your Amazon book URL will not appear on Page One of Google all by itself. It will require On Page and Off Page optimization help. In the interest of transparency, there are many variables that come into play when ranking a webpage on Page One of Google's organic search results. In fact, we wrote the book on search engine optimization entitled **Green Eggs and Google: SEO for the CEO**.

Publicity/PR Campaign: Positive publicity provides a valuable third party endorsement that further builds your trust and credibility in the eyes of prospective patients. Cultivating offline word-of-mouth and accelerating buzz is critical in this day and age because it helps separate you from your competition. Perception equals reality. The more you are featured and quoted in the news media, the more you are perceived as THE expert and authority. If you are perceived as a celebrity surgeon or famous to some degree, prospective patients can mentally justify paying a premium for your healthcare solutions. Here is the prospective patient's thought process: The news media only interviews experts...Experts cost more because they are better...I need an expert for my surgery so I look perfect and feel amazing...I can afford to pay expert fees for the best health outcome possible...Where do I sign?

Our firm will conduct an aggressive PR / Media Relations Campaign on behalf of you and your book. In addition to writing and distributing news releases, we will brainstorm and create innovative "news angles" and story ideas to pitch to targeted journalists and editors.

Besides building your practice brand, enhancing your personal brand and reinforcing your medical guru status in your metro area, each time you are featured or quoted in print, TV or radio, an extraordinary "earned" instead of "paid" media opportunity is produced. This generates web traffic and phone inquiries which often result in new patients.

We've performed these book publishing and book marketing services so many times for our clients that we've been able to streamline the process. Instead of wasting weeks and even months of your time trying to manage everything on your own, it just makes sense to leverage our experience and expertise to ensure that everything runs smoothly and that the outcome is absolutely extraordinary and unforgettable.

www.PlasticSurgeonMarketingMotto.com

"Since I wrote my book on plastic surgery, I am being interviewed on Good Morning America tomorrow."

Scan this QR Code to share with colleagues.

QUALITY CONTROL

A LTHOUGH WE'VE DEVELOPED A SYSTEM for book production, don't think for a minute that this means we cut any corners in the process.

Each custom book we write is unique and exceptionally written based on the transcripts of our client interviews.

This is important, not just because it gives you a book with real worth, but because Amazon checks book submissions carefully and will reject anything that smacks of canned or duplicate content.

To give you an idea of the level of quality control we employ, below is a genuine blueprint for the stages of book production.

Outline And Themes

One of our editorial directors, the person who interviews you during the five one-hour sessions, creates a brief executive summary of your book. This summary guides our ghostwriters on what topics to focus on for the book outline. The executive summary also educates the ghostwriter on the specific results you want to achieve after the prospective patient reads your book. Our ghostwriters read the transcripts through several times and clearly understand the themes and teaching points. If necessary the writer will go online and do additional research on your website to ensure he or she fully understands your procedures, philosophy, equipment and technology.

The next step is to give thought to how the material should be organized to best effect. Which are the most interesting talking points? Which discussions will best motivate the reader? Which anecdotes will be most enjoyable and offer the best fit for the overall theme of the book?

All of this information then has to be put in order so that an outline for the book can be created. Thought has to be given, not just to the logical construction of arguments, but also a flow that will encourage the reader to keep turning the pages.

Style And Form

Now the outline is ready, the writer can begin writing the content, but first he needs to get a feel for your personality and style of speech. Some of this can be gleaned from the transcript and audio recordings but the writer will also take the time to study your website and, if available, videos of you speaking.

This is where ghostwriting becomes an art form. Writing in a manner that reflects the personality of the client, rather than the personality of the writer, is extremely challenging but is something our professional ghostwriters can accomplish with an almost uncanny level of accuracy.

At its most effective, you'll read portions of your book and be unable to shake the feeling that you must have written certain sections yourself and simply forgotten.

Creative Content

Our ghostwriters work quickly, completing up to a 15,000 word book in as little as four to six weeks. But

QUALITY CONTROL

that doesn't mean your content is churned out with little thought or care.

Quite the opposite.

Our ghostwriters care a great a deal about the quality of their work and invest a great deal of time and effort into crafting your book to be the best it can possibly be.

It's not a case of simply rewriting the transcripts into structured sentences and paragraphs; the content has to be creative and imaginative so that the eventual readers can connect with it. It's also essential to ensure that terminology is chosen that enables the average reader to understand it, rather than confusing people with dense, indecipherable medical jargon.

And, as an added bonus, our ghostwriters also have marketing experience which helps greatly in writing content that motivates the reader into action.

Editing And Proofreading

After the first draft is completed, we review it and, if necessary, request adjustments or additions.

The final step is to have the text reviewed by, not one, but two independent proofreaders. This is a crucial step because it ensures maximum accuracy and saves you the embarrassment of pedantic patients pointing out typos.

It's also a matter of professionalism. People expect someone of your education to produce a book that is as free from errors as humanly possible. Our proofreaders are experts in vocabulary and spelling, and know even the most arcane rules of grammar.

The above steps are not an extreme example that only applies to favored clients. This is the same procedure that is carried out for every client and represents the same level of care and quality control that we will apply to the creation of your book.

When we said that we take care of everything… that was no exaggeration.

And there's one other thing we haven't mentioned yet. We also make it ridiculously simple to tap into the power of co-authorship…

www.PlasticSurgeonMarketingMotto.com

Scan this QR Code to share with colleagues.

ONE BOOK = MANY BOOKS

OUR SERVICE IS TAILORED TO your specific requirements.

If you want an audio version of your book, we'll create a recording using a professional voiceover artist... if you do not wish to personalize the audio book with your own voice.

If you want to produce a longer book, we'll accommodate any length you require (it just requires additional interview sessions and more ghostwriting time).

And if you want to co-author your book with two other "Doctor Author Experts," all you have to do is put us in contact and we'll handle everything.

In fact, this third option is something we recommend to all of our clients. Remember, it takes no additional work on your part, but it instantly triples the marketing reach and effect of your book.

It also increases the flow of those crucial referrals because your co-authors are providing you with direct and indirect endorsements of you and your services.

If you need to, go back and reread the chapter entitled "Two's Company...Three's Good Business Sense" to be reminded of why this is such an innovative part of our book publishing strategy.

We've been holding back a little.

Not because we wanted to withhold valuable information from you but because, if we'd talked about this earlier, you might have dismissed it as too demanding.

You see, when you combine your book with that of two other doctors you're not creating one book... you're actually creating three.

Think about it for a moment.

Even though the book is going to contain the work of three doctors, it's natural for each contributor to want their picture and name to be most prominent and for their portion to be the first of the three featured texts.

So, that's what we provide.

Each doctor has their 12,000 to 15,000 word book published, individually, in a digital format.

We then create **THREE DIFFERENT VERSIONS** of the hardback book.

The order of the text inside each book is different and each one has a different cover.

For example…

Dr. Tom writes a plastic surgery book on face lifts, Dr. Dick writes a book on cosmetic dentistry and Dr. Harry writes a book on dermatology.

The cover of Dr. Tom's book features him most prominently and the contents are ordered so that his book comes first, followed by Dr. Dick and Dr. Harry.

The cover of Dr. Dick's book features him most prominently and the contents are ordered so that his book comes first, followed by Dr. Harry and Dr. Tom.

The cover of Dr. Harry's book features him most prominently and the contents are ordered so that his book comes first, followed by Dr. Tom and Dr. Dick.

Got it?

This way everyone gets equal billing and their own version of the book is unique to them.

None of this takes any extra work on your part or your colleagues. As you'd expect, we handle all of the integration and the creation of the different versions of the book.

In fact, your only job is to find two other doctors you want to work with, ask for their permission for us to contact them, and we'll handle everything else.

Don't worry too much about selling the published author opportunity with your colleagues. Just give them the gist of the idea...enough to get them excited about the possibilities. Then, direct them to our book's website located at **PlasticSurgeonMarketingMotto.com** or forward them the link for our educational video presentation at **www.PatientGettingWebinar.com**. If they wish to proceed, we'll go through all the details with them when our scheduled call occurs.

And if one of your local colleagues doesn't go for the idea, no problem...just approach someone else. You'll actually be amazed how easy it is to find two local colleagues who will recognize the value of what you all can achieve.

There are so many benefits to co-authorship but here are a couple more we haven't mentioned yet.

Reduce Costs By Up To 66%: Creating a book long enough to be suitable for printed publication involves a greater expense than producing a single, short Amazon Kindle book. But when three of you combine your books together, you can also share the hard costs three ways and make the whole project more affordable for everyone (although, as we've already mentioned, there's nothing to stop you from taking on someone else's costs to encourage their cooperation – no one's going to turn down the opportunity to become a published author when you're offering to cover all of their publishing costs).

100 Free Hardback Books: In addition to the 100 free hardcover books we include in the package, we'll give you an extra 100 hardcover books for each book project that you refer us to (including your own). If you're selling your hardcover book for $26, that represents over $2,600 of free books for you to give away as you see fit.

Now can you see why it makes so much sense to go down the co-authorship route?

Good. So here's where we blow your mind just a little bit.

There is absolutely no reason why you need to stop at just one compendium. You can repeat this process with as many doctors as you like…

Still using the same book that you've created.

Crack open your rolodex and work your way through all the people who referred you new patients, trained with in medical school, worked for at one time, know through study clubs or met at conferences.

As long as they work in a different specialty or in a sufficiently distant geographical area, they're a potential book partner. Just give them a call and introduce the idea.

Once you've produced one book and seen the benefits, you'll be hooked. When you decide that you want to be published in yet another book, and you know that all you have to do is make a few phone calls to set the ball rolling, you won't be able to contain yourself.

Partner up with a dozen different colleagues and your book will be circulating among the doctors' offices, patients' homes, waiting rooms, reception areas, media contacts and patient-to-patient referrals of **12 different doctors!**

You can reduce the level of resistance still further by partnering up with a doctor who is also keen to be published far and wide. If the two of you combine your books, every time you find one new doctor or surgeon to work with you will already have enough content to produce a brand new book.

And, of course, we'll happily provide you with another 100 free hardback copies of your book for every new doctor you work with.

Look, you might be perfectly content to produce just one compendium and reap the benefits for years to come. But if your aspirations are bigger, we really couldn't make it any easier to spread your book wider and farther than you could ever have imagined. We call our innovative approach the ultimate in offline viral marketing for your practice.

www.PlasticSurgeonMarketingMotto.com

"Oh no, another practice management consultant that promises us salvation."

Scan this QR Code to share with colleagues.

THE BOTTOM LINE:

HE WHO HESITATES

www.PlasticSurgeonMarketingMotto.com

"Since Joe Preston and Phil Guye helped you write and publish THE book on plastic surgery, it is now time to address your fans and new patients."

Scan this QR Code to share with colleagues.

ONE MORE THING

REGARDLESS OF THE SPECIFIC AREA of plastic surgery that your book covers, the final chapter of your book will be the "call to action."

You're going to thank your reader for taking the time to enjoy your book.

You're going to remind them of the main health and wellness points that they must remember above all else.

And then you're going to ask them to do one thing: to take the one supremely important action that every chapter preceding has been subtly – or overtly – leading the readers towards.

This could be as simple as visiting your practice or website. But it's more likely to be along the lines of agreeing to a specific treatment or procedure.

It's not enough to hint or gently cajole; your final chapter should give the reader one final push into the direction you believe is best for their physical as well as mental health and wellness. Remind them of the benefits of acting now and remind them of the dangers of procrastination.

But you need to do more than that.

Simply restating the main points isn't going to get the job done.

You need to construct an argument, remind the reader of the impending pain, help them to visualize the achieved outcome and the benefits of taking the right course and...

And...

Introduce a previously unrevealed fact that pushes any fence-sitters over the edge.

The best way to help you understand how to achieve all of this is to use a practical example. So, imagine that you've just read a scintillating and ground-breaking exploration of how becoming a published author can revolutionize your medical practice. The following is how we would motivate you to take the desired next step (the text in brackets indicates the various points you want to try to hit in your final chapter).

{THE EXCITING POSSIBILITIES} The healthcare industry is an exciting place to be right now. The advances in technology have opened up a range of desirable and profitable treatment options that allow patients to improve their health and aesthetics without having to worry about unmanageable pain and extended recovery periods.

{HERE COMES THE PAIN} But that isn't to say that those working in the industry don't have their challenges.

Competition for profitable patients is intense. And even the most experienced and successful plastic surgeons are finding themselves losing ground through price wars and a dangerous breed of less-than-scrupulous practitioners offering discounted prices.

Whether you're experiencing this problem already, or it's something you expect to face in the very near future, this situation isn't going to resolve itself. Sitting back and simply hoping that the people in your community will make the smart choices is a recipe for disaster.

{HERE'S THE LIGHT AT THE END OF THE TUNNEL} But there is a solution...

A solution that will secure your flow of referrals

and new patients, not just in the short-term but in the long-term as well.

One simple marketing push now, and you'll be reaping the benefits for years and years to come.

And here's the really good news...

It's so easy and fast to do that if you get started today, you could have this marketing strategy up and running in about 90 days.

{IMAGINE THE BENEFITS} By now, of course, you realize that we're talking about the power of becoming a published author. The benefits are almost endless...

- Co-author with other surgeons, doctors or professionals so you can widen your marketing reach and receive more referrals.

- Educate your prospective patients so they recognize you as THE Authority and schedule surgery with you.

- Leave your hard cover book in the waiting room so your prospective patients see you as a published author   and increase their trust in your expertise.

- Give your hard cover book to patients as a gift

so they're more likely to remain lifetime customers AND recommend you to others.

- Use the book to answer frequently asked questions about pain management and recovery so you can eliminate the #1 reason why patients delay or decline surgery.

- Publish your book on Amazon properly so you can dominate Page One of Google and generate more patient leads.

- Send your book to the news media so you can get interviewed by journalists and earn free publicity...helping you become a recognized local celebrity.

- Give your book to event organizers so you can seize valuable speaking opportunities.

We could go on and on but surely, by now, you can see the wisdom of this approach.

This isn't one marketing tactic – it's an entire series of marketing strategies rolled into one.

{BUT THERE'S A SNAG} The only downside is the

learning curve that comes with taking your book from conception to publication.

{**WITH AN EASY SOLUTION**} But that downside is **COMPLETELY REMOVED** if you utilize our "done for you" service. All you have to do is commit five hours of your time for the interviews and, in about 90 days, your book will be published online and 100 hardcover copies will be on their way to your office.

{**VISUALIZE IT!**} Imagine the excitement of holding your book in your hand, and the satisfaction of personally signing books for your prospective patients, existing patients, staff, colleagues, and for your family and friends.

"Thanks for coming in Mrs. Jones, it's been great to see you. Before you go, I've got some really exciting news. I recently finished writing my first book and the first copies arrived yesterday. I'd love to give you a copy to take home. Perhaps you can tell me what you think the next time you come in." This doesn't have to be something that you might get around to eventually. Turn the key today and we'll get started and have the job finished in about 90 days.

{BUILD CONFIDENCE} Rest assured that your project will be in the safest of hands. Our marketing expertise has been utilized by a whole range of clients, from doctors to Fortune 500 companies.

{TESTIMONIALS} And the doctors who have already used our marketing services have been thrilled with the results.

"Anyone in the healthcare industry with an MD or an MBA after their name needs to read Plastic Surgeon Marketing Motto. Joe Preston and Phil Guye have created one of the most innovative referral and patient getting systems ever developed."
-Dr. Steve Vasilev, MD, MBA

"If you only read one book about marketing your medical practice this year, this is the one. Phil Guye and Joe Preston are authorities on how to influence and persuade prospects and convert them into patients."
-Dr. Kim Millman, MD, PhD

"Joe, Phil and their staff streamline a potentially time-consuming, difficult and tedious process thereby making it extremely efficient and manageable. The vision and marketing prowess of Mr. Preston and Mr. Guye comes alive in the book writing process making it a pleasure to work with them."
-Dr. Jason Stoner, DDS, MS

"Joe and Phil and their team were very easy to work with and made writing a book for my practice very easy. Their services have helped to separate my business from our competitors. I highly recommend Joe Preston and Phil Guye and their firm DoctorBookPublishing.com."
-Dr. Mark F. Hardison, DDS

"Joe Preston and Phil Guye are the consummate professionals. They have really used their expertise in the areas of marketing and media training and media coaching to help me convey my message in the strongest way possible to my patients. I'm glad that we did because it really helps me to this day."
-Dr. David Scharf, DMD

"I couldn't say enough great things about Joe Preston and Phil Guye. I mean, in a really short amount of time, I feel like they are my long lost brothers. They are committed guys, hardworking much like myself, maybe that's why we connect. They are all about the bottom line and we need to get the job done no matter what it takes, we're going to get the job done and that's how I am. No matter how long the day is, we're going to get it done and we're going to make it right and we're going to make it happen and we're going to make it a success. So, I'm very happy and fortunate, really to have met them and connected with them and I'm very, very satisfied with their ex-cellent, beyond excellent, service and expertise."

-Dr. Ed De Endrade, DDS

"First thing I want to say about Joe and Phil is that they are very - I want to use the word as a doctor would say patient-centered. But they are very client-centered. Joe and Phil frame and posi-tion you and they do the framing of the market-ing before the patient even arrives in your office."

-Dr. Coury Staadecker, DDS, MS

"One of my biggest concerns before hiring someone to do my SEO number one is that they would be knowledgeable and number two is that they would be able to really deliver the goods and get me on the top of page one and Joe Preston and Phil Guye couldn't be better in both categories. Joe and Phil are virtually the encyclopedia of SEO knowledge and they are always keeping themselves current. And I use them as a resource too because I enjoy SEO myself and I like calling them and bouncing marketing ideas off them or picking their brains. And ever since they have been on my team I've been number one on Google search for all my keywords and that's a real boost for my practice. So, I appreciate the work Joe and Phil have done for me and I really couldn't recommend them more highly."

-Dr. David Scharf, DMD

"Joe Preston and Phil Guye really have an interesting perspective. We are not our patients. Joe and Phil come with an incredible perspective, a different perspective. They see things the way the patient sees it. And that speaks about them for what they are capable of doing for us. That's just an in-

credible, incredible insight into our patients' mind and how is it that we're going to target that patient. What's going to make that patient come to us when they don't even know us. We're on the right track with Joe and Phil and their company."
-Dr. Ed De Endrade, DDS

"I love passion and there is no one more passionate about what they do than Joe Preston and Phil Guye. And they are just dedicated to my success. And for me, not only do I want them to be successful but I want my friends to experience what Joe and Phil have done for me. The effort on my part was not even a blip on my radar screen. And the results have been phenomenal."
-Dr. Jason Stoner, DDS, MS

{WAITING IS DANGEROUS} However, there is one thing we haven't yet mentioned that we weren't sure whether to bring up. But in the interests of transparency we feel it's important to at least make you aware of the limitations that we have.

You see, out of respect for our clients, we pledge to only create and publish a custom book featuring a surgical procedure for **ONE** plastic surgeon in a designated territory.

This is good news for our clients because we offer this type of exclusivity.

The bad news is that your competition may have already beaten you to the punch.

We've developed an educational video presentation located online at **www.GetMorePlasticSurgeryPatients.com** that shows you our method. This webinar is promoted via our book, direct mail, online advertising, email marketing, search engine optimization, speaking engagements and social media.

It's only a matter of time before a plastic surgeon in your region jumps at this opportunity.

The only question is whether that plastic surgeon is you, or your competition.

In other words, you may not want to take too much time coming to a decision.

{ELIMINATE THE RISK} You should know that we provide all of our clients a 30 Day Money Back Guarantee on our publishing system. If for any reason during the first 30 days of our process (which include the five one hour interview calls), you feel our system is

not the right fit for your practice, we will refund 100%
of your investment.

{**CALL TO ACTION**} So, now that you know what's
at stake, all you have to do is...

Get the idea?

In truth you may want to employ a little more subtlety than we have. There's a fair amount of difference
between writing a medical book for a consumer audience and writing a marketing book for a business
audience. A business audience expects a more direct
approach.

But the above should at least give you an idea of
how you may want to close your book.

Not that you need to worry about that if you're
using our "done for you" service because...

Well...

The closing "call to action" in your book will also be
done for you.

Take a quick look at the calendar and note today's
date.

Now count forward three short months.

If you get the ball rolling today, that could be the

date when you first hold your brand new book in your hands.

Ready to go?

All you have to do is to visit our website **PlasticSurgeonApplication.com** and complete the short application. Once you're finished the application, you can use our online scheduling system to book your appointment for the telephone conference call with Phil or Joe. This publishing strategy session will give us the opportunity to discuss the details and make sure that this is a good fit for you and a good fit for us (we prefer to work with ambitious, forward-thinking medical professionals who are cool and not uptight). Before our scheduled conversation, we require a small deposit but this is only to weed out the tire kickers and time vampires. This deposit also secures exclusivity for your book in your designated territory. If you decide after the 30 minute publishing strategy session with us that this isn't for you, your deposit will be refunded within 24 hours, no questions asked.

Thank you for taking the time to read this book. We sincerely hope that you've found it useful and that you will use this system to develop your practice and take it to the next level so you experience your best year ever. We look forward to hearing from you soon and we'll be thrilled by the opportunity to help you become a proud, published author.

By the way, you may be wondering what the title of this book really means. Our Plastic Surgeon Marketing Motto is: "Promote Unto Others So They Will Promote Unto You." In essence, promote your referral partners first and they will refer you more patients. This strategy is simple. It works. It is the secret recipe to grow referrals. Co-authoring your book with two other referring doctors (or professionals) is the most strategic way to Promote Unto Others So They Will Promote Unto You.

ABOUT THE CO-AUTHORS

P HILLIP GUYE AND JOSEPH PRESTON are
Senior Managing Partners of Doctor Reputation
Management (www.DrReputationManagement.com),
a leading marketing solutions firm they co-founded to
provide their clients with the highest level of patient
and customer acquisition success currently available in
the marketplace.

By leveraging the skills and techniques they created and enhanced over 22 years for intensive reputation management, public relations, advanced search engine optimization (SEO) and viral video marketing, Preston, Guye and their team help many of the nation's leading doctors, medical practices and hospitals. Their proprietary "Patient-Getting" formula for creating Patient Indoctrination Videos positively influences prospective patients so that they truly get to Know, Like, Trust and Fall In Love with doctors and their practices before the initial consultation. Phil and Joe are also the co-founders of Doctor Book Publishing, a multi-channel media publishing company dedicated to transforming leading doctors into published authors and media celebrities.

Featured in Forbes magazine, Vanity Fair magazine, Time magazine, USA Today, BusinessWeek Small Biz magazine as well as interviewed on CNN and Fox News, Joseph Preston has helped companies ranging in size from start-ups to the Fortune 500 including The Home Depot, McDonalds, Reebok, Playtex and RedBox.

According to a feature article in Forbes magazine, "Joseph Preston worked a crowd of reporters who gathered at Washington, D.C.'s posh Galileo restaurant and then rushed off to their newsrooms to give Preston airtime...Preston, who has been in public relations since he was 19, managed to plant a story on the cover of USA Today's Life section...Within two days images of Preston aired on the national news and on some 30 local stations...The Sunday Times of London, Time magazine and other print media ran with the story."

As a reputation and PR strategist overseeing the Washington, DC office, Preston has successfully influenced and persuaded journalists from a variety of national media outlets to interview and feature his clientele in The Wall Street Journal, New York Times, Washington Post, Los Angeles Times, Newsweek, Glamour, Elle, InStyle, New York Post, New York Daily News, Associated Press, CBS, ABC, NBC and the Huffington Post. To prepare his clients for media interviews and crisis situations, Joseph Preston conducts intensive media training for CEOs, doctors, attorneys and spokespersons of both large and small organizations.

As a passionate and engaging speaker, Mr. Preston has lectured and presented internationally at various medical, university and corporate events on topics including: patient/customer acquisition strategies, reputation management, public relations, SEO, book publishing, book marketing, patient indoctrination videos and cinematic storytelling.

Phillip Guye has helped companies such as Boeing, Warner Bros., ABC, Nissan, Levi's, Hot Topic, Mercedes Benz, Funny Or Die and College Humor. Utilizing a variety of marketing disciplines, Phil Guye has also worked with celebrities and artists including: 50 Cent, Snoop Dog, Dr. Dre, Rihanna, Pamela Anderson, Ice Cube, Roy Disney, Rip Torn and George Clooney. He oversees the Los Angeles office as well as the firm's green screen and white cyc film studio.

Guye's unique understanding of how to influence prospects to become customers and persuade them to virally endorse these products via social media has created a demand from pharmaceutical companies and sporting goods manufacturers for his strategic counsel on everything from brand positioning to package design as well as new worldwide product launches.

Phillip Guye, a bonafide authority and recognized expert on search engine optimization, has been hired by SEO software companies for his insight on advanced product development and feature enhancements.

Both Phil's and Joe's unique understanding of the

Google algorithm, Google's ever evolving updates and other second tier search engine sensitivities has enabled them to co-author other books including Green Eggs And Google For Kids, Green Eggs And Google: SEO for the CEO and Reputation Management 911: Defuse Online Attackers & Disarm Dishonest Competitors. Preston and Guye are also the co-authors of four medical marketing books including: Dental Marketing Motto, Doctor Marketing Motto, Orthopedic Surgeon Marketing Motto and Plastic Surgeon Marketing Motto.

ADDITIONAL BOOKS BY
PHILLIP GUYE AND JOSEPH PRESTON

Green Eggs And Google:
SEO for the CEO

Reputation Management 911:
Defuse Online Attackers
&
Disarm Dishonest Competitors

Green Eggs And Google For Kids

QUESTIONS TO ASK
PHIL GUYE, JOE PRESTON
OR THEIR STAFF

_____

_____

_____

_____

_____

_____

_____

_____

_____

_____

_____

_____

_____

_____

_____

_____

QUESTIONS TO ASK
PHIL GUYE, JOE PRESTON
OR THEIR STAFF

_____

_____

_____

_____

_____

_____

_____

_____

_____

_____

_____

_____

_____

_____

_____

_____

_____

QUESTIONS TO ASK
PHIL GUYE, JOE PRESTON
OR THEIR STAFF

_____

_____

_____

_____

_____

_____

_____

_____

_____

_____

_____

_____

_____

_____

_____

_____

_____

QUESTIONS TO ASK PHIL GUYE, JOE PRESTON OR THEIR STAFF

QUESTIONS TO ASK
PHIL GUYE, JOE PRESTON
OR THEIR STAFF

_____

_____

_____

_____

_____

_____

_____

_____

_____

_____

_____

_____

_____

_____

_____

QUESTIONS TO ASK PHIL GUYE, JOE PRESTON OR THEIR STAFF

_____

_____

_____

_____

_____

_____

_____

_____

_____

_____

_____

_____

_____

_____

_____

_____

_____

_____

QUESTIONS TO ASK
PHIL GUYE, JOE PRESTON
OR THEIR STAFF

_____

_____

_____

_____

_____

_____

_____

_____

_____

_____

_____

_____

_____

_____

QUESTIONS TO ASK
PHIL GUYE, JOE PRESTON
OR THEIR STAFF

_____

_____

_____

_____

_____

_____

_____

_____

_____

_____

_____

_____

_____

_____

_____

_____

_____

_____

QUESTIONS TO ASK
PHIL GUYE, JOE PRESTON
OR THEIR STAFF

_____

_____

_____

_____

_____

_____

_____

_____

_____

_____

_____

_____

_____

_____

_____

_____

_____

QUESTIONS TO ASK
PHIL GUYE, JOE PRESTON
OR THEIR STAFF

QUESTIONS TO ASK
PHIL GUYE, JOE PRESTON
OR THEIR STAFF

_____

_____

_____

_____

_____

_____

_____

_____

_____

_____

_____

_____

_____

_____

_____

_____

_____

QUESTIONS TO ASK PHIL GUYE, JOE PRESTON OR THEIR STAFF

_____

_____

_____

_____

_____

_____

_____

_____

_____

_____

_____

_____

_____

_____

_____

_____

_____

www.ingramcontent.com/pod-product-compliance
Lightning Source LLC
Chambersburg PA
CBHW021555210326
41599CB00010B/460